9-20

Izzie MacColl

ALATEEN
—a day at a time

Al-Anon Family Group Headquarters, Inc.
VIRGINIA

Al-Anon Family Group Headquarters, Inc.
1600 C-

Website www.al-anonuk.org.uk
Email enquiries@al-anonuk.org.uk   5
Fax 020 7378 9910

Al-Anon/Alateen is supported by members' voluntary contributions and from the sale of our Conference Approved Literature.

Library of Congress Catalog Card No. 83-070348
ISBN-978-0-910034-53-1

Publisher's Cataloging in Publication

Alateen—a day at a time.
  p. cm.
  Includes index.
  LCCN 83-070348.
  ISBN 978-0-910034-53-1

1. Children of alcoholics—Miscellanea 2. Youth—Family relationships—Miscellanea 3. Alcoholics—Family relationships. 4. Alcoholics—Rehabilitation—United States. 5. Al-Anon Family Group Headquarters, inc. 6. Alcoholics Anonymous. I. Al-Anon Family Group Headquarters, inc.

HV5133.A43 1989   362.292'3
                                         QB192-20139

Approved by
World Service Conference
Al-Anon Family Groups

Alateen, part of the Al-Anon Family Groups, is a fellowship of young people whose lives have been affected by alcoholism in a family member or close friend. We help each other by sharing our experience, strength, and hope.

We believe alcoholism is a family disease because it affects all the members emotionally and sometimes physically. Although we cannot change or control our parents, we can detach from their problems while continuing to love them.

We do not discuss religion or become involved with any outside organizations. Our sole topic is the solution of our problems. We are always careful to protect each other's anonymity as well as that of all Al-Anon and A.A. members.

By applying the Twelve Steps to ourselves, we begin to grow mentally, emotionally, and spiritually. We will always be grateful to Alateen for giving us a wonderful, healthy program to live by and enjoy.

The Suggested Alateen Preamble to the Twelve Steps

INTRODUCTION

The following pages enfold, day by day, the personal sharings of Alateen members from around the world. Some are unique experiences; many are familiar to each of us. They all capture the struggle of our experience in living with the problem of alcoholism, the strength we've found in the program, and the hope we feel sharing with others who understand.

The message of this collection of thoughts is simple: "Yesterday is gone and tomorrow isn't here, so I can only live for today." If we take time to think about that, we won't have time for past regrets and worries about the future. We'll be too busy getting the most out of life, a day at a time.

Another new year begins. What's in it for me? Will it be a time when I make a lot of promises only to see them broken before the month barely begins? Or will it be a time for a fresh start?

With the help of the program, it can be a new beginning. It's a time to let go of the resentments and hurts I've been carrying around and a time to look more honestly at myself.

Maybe I'll start with a slogan or take a look at a Step. Or maybe I'll get to know a new person. I'll try to work hard at the program, one day at a time, and find that new spark of energy that will help me to grow.

Things to Think About

Today is a chance to make a new start. I'll take a closer look at the program and really try to get at what it means in my life. I'll let go of the past and look ahead with a positive attitude. I know it's going to be a great year!

I came to Alateen because I couldn't cope with the drinking of someone close to me. But is this the reason I keep coming back?

If I think about it, Alateen probably means a lot more to me than just learning to live with alcoholism. It's a fellowship where I can meet other teenagers who have problems just like mine. It's a place where I can be open and honest about how I feel. And, most of all, Alateen is a program that helps me in all parts of my life—at home, at school, with my friends, and with myself.

Things to Think About

Alateen not only helps me to handle the trouble that comes from living with alcoholism; it gives me a chance to do something about every part of my life. Practicing the program "in all my affairs" will help me to get the most out of life today.

I'm going through a stage of my life when change is the name of the game. My body is changing. I feel different, too. Some days I'm moody; others, I'm awkward and embarrassed. Sometimes I feel on top of the world.

With all these changes to think about, it's hard to cope with the changes at home, too. Things are up and down. It seems as if every day there's something different to deal with.

Alateen is helping me to make sense of these changes in my life. Being with other teenagers who live with an alcoholic helps me to realize that I'm not alone. We're all going through the same kinds of changes—and we're doing it together.

Things to Thinks About

Being a teenager isn't easy. Neither is living with an alcoholic. When you put them together, you can have double trouble. But today, with the help of the program, I'm learning to cope.

Before I came to Alateen I was reliving yesterday and worrying about tomorrow. That left me no time for today. I was in a daze all the time and I didn't know what I was doing.

Then I was lucky enough to discover Alateen. At first I was hardheaded and stuck to my old ways. But now, after some time in the program, I'm realizing that the best way to live is "One Day at a Time." Sometimes, when things get tough, I even have to live one minute at a time.

I know I don't have to worry about what's coming tomorrow or what I did yesterday. With the help of my Higher Power and the program, I can live for today and enjoy it.

Things to Think About

Yesterday is gone and tomorrow isn't here, so I can only live for today. If I worry about what's going to happen or what's already happened, I'll forget to be thankful for what I have now. Alateen keeps me on track and helps me to live "One Day at a Time."

How my day goes depends on how I see my problems. If I think of them as stumbling blocks, I'll probably be uptight and frustrated. But if I try to use my problems as stepping-stones to find out more about myself, today can be an important step in my growth.

Admitting I'm wrong can be a stepping-stone to being honest and humble. Working on an assignment I've put off can make me more responsible. Letting go of one of my fears can help me find faith in a Higher Power.

Stepping-stones or stumbling blocks—the choice is mine.

Things to Think About

No one can tell me how I should feel about today. That right belongs to me alone. I'll be a lot further ahead if I don't let my problems get me down. They *can* make me stronger today if I use them to dig deeper into the program.

When I had a hard time handling things that were happening around me, I used to run away into my own little dreamworld. It kept me from hurting so much. I'd dream about being a movie star or a hero or just about being special in someone else's life.

In the program I'm learning to face reality instead of dreaming my life away. The Steps and slogans are helping me see things as they are and deal with the hurt I feel.

I'm still a dreamer, but that's okay because now I know the difference between what's real and what's a dream. My dreams can help me look on the brighter side of things as long as I don't lose sight of what's really happening in my life today.

Things to Think About

I'm free to dream, but *how* I dream can make a big difference to what happens in my life. Instead of escaping to dreamland, I can use the program to be realistic about things and let my dreams help me to be a positive thinker today.

After my first few Alateen meetings I started to read some of the literature. At first I thought most of what I read wasn't for me. The Steps and Traditions were confusing and the slogans seemed too simple.

After awhile I noticed that I was living by the slogans; I just hadn't recognized the words. I had my own translations. "Live and Let Live," for example, was Give a little, take a little.

I've thought of other slogans to express the program: Think and say thanks, I found a friend, Make the most of it. But making them up isn't nearly as important as living by them. That's what I'm trying to do today.

Things to Think About

To keep things simple, I'll stick to the slogans. The words and ideas are easy enough to understand, but when they're put into action, they have the power to change my life.

I felt like smashing the world into little pieces. My mother was always drunk and I was sure she didn't care what happened to me. I wanted to yell at the top of my lungs, but I just boiled inside instead.

When I came to Alateen, I learned that I can't do anything about my mother's drinking. She's sick and she'll get help only when she's ready. But I *can* do something about my own feelings. I can let out my anger instead of holding it in, knowing that people in Alateen will understand and accept me. And instead of trying to smash the world, I can use the program to break down my big problems into little ones. That makes a lot more sense to me!

Things to Think About

Sometimes I get so mad I want to scream. There's nothing wrong with that, but where and when I express my anger can make a difference. A good place to do it is at a meeting where it will fall on ears that understand. Those ears belong to people who are ready to help me track the anger to its source and find a positive and healthy way to deal with it.

When I was younger, I had a personal idea of God: a Higher Power who knew my problems and was ready to help me. I didn't think of Him every day, but I knew He was there when I needed Him.

Then, as the alcoholism in our home got worse, I started to feel as if God had turned against me. I blamed Him when things went wrong—when I had trouble with my schoolwork and when my friends didn't understand why things in my home were different from theirs.

The program helped me get back the feeling I once had for God. Instead of my old negative way of blaming God for my troubles, I can turn to Him now for help. I don't always get what I ask for, but it's better that I don't. God knows better than I do what's good for me, and that's the way I like it!

Things to Think About

I make things harder for me when I block my Higher Power out. It's a lonely and scary feeling trying to work things out on my own. When I learn to trust and ask my Higher Power for help, things have a way of going a lot better. The program always gives me the choice, but I think I'll stick with my Higher Power, in order to work my problems out with Someone who cares.

I went to my first meeting with my fists clenched. I was angry, frustrated, and ready to fight with anyone.

I realize now that was just a cover for all the pain I was feeling. Something inside me felt raw, like a well-chewed bone, and I really just wanted to run away from everything.

That's when the miracle of the fellowship happened to me. The pain I had felt turned into a tool to help others when I reached out to a newcomer and said, "I know how you feel because I've been there." It was the truth then and it's the truth now. Sharing my pain was the key to freedom for me.

Things to Think About

I had a lot of pain in my past. At one time I thought it would kill me. Now I'm glad I experienced it because I'm able to reach out to others and let them know I understand how they feel. That message was loud and clear when I came into Alateen and I want to carry it to others.

When we first come to Alateen it's hard for some of us to see how dishonest we've become. If we don't steal or tell lies, we think we've being honest. But there are other ways of being dishonest with ourselves.

Some of us hide our real feelings of loneliness and fear by getting into trouble, refusing friendship, or even studying to try and outsmart other people. We try to tell ourselves and others that this is the way we want to live, but deep down inside we know we're not being honest; we're only hurting ourselves.

We learn in the program that we don't have to live this way. We can stop hiding behind our lies and tell it like it really is. As we get honest about our feelings, it's a lot easier to live with ourselves and the people around us.

Things to Think About

In Alateen I don't have to fake it because I'm not afraid to show my real feelings. Being honest about myself makes me feel a lot better because other people get to know me as I really am. After all, cover-ups are no substitute for the real ME.

When my parents didn't give me the kind of attention I was looking for, I accused them of not loving me at all and turned my back on them. When I came to the fellowship, I found out how wrong I'd been. Instead of accepting what they had to offer, I rejected it.

Working the program helped me to understand that everyone loves in a different way. When I stopped expecting my parents to love me on my terms, I was better able to accept them and their feelings for me. It didn't take long for me to realize that they've never stopped loving me at all.

Things to Think About

Other people may not be capable of loving me the way I want to be loved. Can I accept that without resentment and still love them? I can if I'm willing to accept them as they are and remember that real love comes with no strings attached.

Sometimes I like to take the easy way out; I do the things I want to do, not the things I have to do. It's more fun to go out with my friends than to do the homework I've been putting off for hours; it's easier to sit around the house instead of doing my chores.

When I feel like doing what I want instead of what I need to do, I'll remember "First Things First." If I take the slogan seriously, it will help me to decide what *is* important. When I've taken care of my responsibilities to myself and to others, I'll have a lot more time to enjoy the things I like to do.

Things to Think About

What's important in my life? What do I want? What do I need? Alateen helps me to answer these questions. To keep my priorities straight, I'll put "First Things First" today.

Before I came to Alateen, life didn't make much sense to me. I didn't understand why people had to hurt each other the way they did. I didn't know what to expect, who to trust, or which way to turn.

That confusion really got to me. I was trying to tackle all my problems at once. I was frustrated and sometimes felt like giving up.

But being confused made me dig deeper into the program to set things straight. The Twelve Steps helped me sort things out a little bit at a time. Gradually my thinking got back on track and life started to make a lot more sense.

Things to Think About

Alateen is the key which unlocks the door of my confused mind. I have a program that helps me to make sense of my mixed-up thinking and feeling. Living it will show me how to find some peace of mind for today.

The First Step tells me I am powerless over alcohol—what it does to the person who drinks it or how much he drinks. In fact, I have no control over any other person. If I'm spending a lot of time trying to control others, then I'm letting my own life get out of control. My life has become unmanageable.

If I can accept the fact that *I* am the only person that I can change, then I won't have to deal with feelings of guilt and fear which come when I try to control the alcoholic and other people in my life. I can get on with living my own life.

Things to Think About

Acceptance is the biggest part of the First Step. It's the beginning of me being in control of my own life again. I can have that control today if I work at putting Step One into practice.

There were times before Alateen when I didn't know what to say to people. I wanted them to know that I really cared about them, but nothing came out. I knew they were ready to listen to me, but something kept me from saying how I really felt.

Today I'm learning to keep it simple. I don't worry about the words; I just try to tell people how I feel. I say, "I think that's great!" or "I really don't like that." I try to mean what I say. I don't worry that they won't like hearing what I have to say. I tell the truth because I want to be honest with myself and the people I'm talking to.

Things to Think About

Feelings are just as important as words when I'm trying to say something. The problem helps me to be honest about my feelings and to "tell it like it is." Today I'll try to keep the words simple and let my feelings do the talking.

Many people ask, "How do I find God?" The answer comes through searching, listening, and learning through other people's experiences.

I believe God is inside each of us. My God is loving. He wants only what's good for me. He helps me feel good about myself. I believe in Him because I've seen Him in my Alateen friends.

How I feel during the day has a lot to do with doing God's will. When I try to run things my own way, I end up feeling terrible. But if I try to live each day to the best of my ability, doing what God wants me to do, I feel a lot better.

Things to Think About

In Alateen I've found a Power greater than myself. He loves me and He gives me the strength to get through each day. I believe in Him and I know He believes in me.

My thoughts and feelings are like a cake mix; the ingredients can be great, but they aren't much good until they're blended together and have a shape to be poured into. I can have lots of good thoughts and feelings, but if my actions don't tell the same story, they're wasted.

I choose what kind of shape I give to my thoughts and feelings by the way I act each day. When I try to manage things by myself, I end up in sad shape. Some days I think I can control situations in my life, but really I can't.

Step Three has a better way. Turning my will (my thoughts and feelings) *and* my life (my actions) over to the care of God as I understand Him, gives me a stronger, healthier life. When my thoughts and feelings and my actions work together in harmony, "the recipe" has a better chance for success.

Things to Think About

How I think and feel is an important part of me; so is the way I act. But if my thoughts and feelings don't connect with my actions, I'm in trouble. Step Three can help make the connection stronger. It shows me how to let God take care of my will and my life so I can act in a more positive way each day.

The cofounder of A.A., Bill W., discovered that in desperate moments the only way he could regain serenity was to reach out and help another troubled alcoholic. In Alateen we have the opportunity to help others every day.

By reaching out and sharing our experiences with other members of the group, we can help them understand and deal with their problems. In doing this, we actually get more than we give. We see them grow and it helps us to grow as well.

This kind of help isn't teaching or preaching; it's the sharing of experience, strength, and hope. It's opening myself up and letting other people in.

Things to Think About

The more I reach out to others, the more I see my own needs and strengths. My thoughts and feelings become a little clearer and I start to find solutions to my own problems while I'm helping others deal with theirs. Reaching out is caring for others *and* myself in a special way. Today I'll reach out and let myself get close to people.

When I first heard people talking about acceptance and surrender at a meeting, I thought they were crazy and I told them so. Surely they didn't expect me to roll over and play dead and let people walk over me. I'd been at war with the alcoholic forever, it seemed, and there was no way I was going to give in now and let him win.

When I finally quieted down, someone got through to me. She helped me realize that I'd made a real mess of my life by trying to control and change everybody around me. That hit me hard and made me stop and think.

Now I know there are some things I just can't change, especially other people. Admitting that isn't easy. But I realize that when I surrender and accept this, I'm not the weak person I thought I'd be; I'm a lot stronger. I'm not hopelessly giving up—I'm just trying to let go of the things I can't change, in order to get on with changing myself.

Things to Think About

Acceptance and surrender are attitudes that open doors to living. When I let go of my stubborn self-will and accept the fact that I can't control everything and everyone in my life, it's a big step in my own growth. It gives me time to work on me and that's the real purpose of the program.

When I was only in Alateen a few months, I kept asking my friends if they'd noticed a change for the better in me. I felt happier and more serene, but I still wanted others to tell me that the program was helping me to recover.

What I didn't realize then was that I didn't need the approval of other people to flatter my ego.

I'm getting better now. I'm starting to feel right about what I do as I let *my* conscience be my guide. If I keep coming to Alateen meetings with an open mind, my Higher Power will take it from there.

Things to Think About

I can listen to and accept the good things people say about me, but I don't have to go looking for them to make myself feel better. I know I'm living the program as well as I can, one day at a time. That's the best reason I can think of for feeling good about myself.

It's not easy to admit that sometimes I do things that are mean. I pick fights because it makes me feel good to yell and there are times that I really hate people. Who wants to tell anyone things like that?

It's hard to keep carrying this stuff around, but Step Five—admitting to God, myself, and another person—helps me to get it out. When I admit these feelings I can let them go and get them out of my head which helps me feel free!

Things to Think About

Step Five is a great relief! It's good not to have to hide my feelings inside anymore. Getting things out in the open by admitting my faults clears my mind and makes it easier to think about getting the most out of today.

God has a lot of patience with us as we stumble around trying to become better people. Sometimes after Step Five we want to hold on to a few pet faults. We know we have to let go of them, but we're just not ready.

Step Six can help. It's not a very lengthy Step but is says a lot. God will help us when we're ready to *give up* the struggle to do our own will. It's another way to "Let Go and Let God" take over the reins.

Things to Think About

Step Six is my chance to cooperate with God. My goal is to make myself ready to let go of my faults and let God take care of the rest.

When things went from bad to worse at home, I started running away. When I did return, my mother couldn't trust me; she never knew what I was going to do. So she stayed home with me and I couldn't go anywhere. I'd behave for awhile; then when she'd start letting me go out, I'd do the same things all over again.

One time when I came home, I was physically sick from all my running around. That's when my mother spoke to me about Al-Anon and Alateen. She caught me at the right moment because I would have tried anything to stop feeling so bad.

The next night I went to my first meeting and saw, in action, what she'd described to me. For the first time I felt like staying in one place. I came out of the meeting feeling better and I knew that instead of running away, I could come back here and work out my problems with people who understand.

Things to Think About

It seems easy enough to run away from my problems, but they usually follow me wherever I go. It takes more courage to deal with them face to face. When I use the program to do that, I never stand alone. There's a fellowship of friends waiting to welcome me and help me find the solutions I need.

When I was younger, I thought life was peaches and cream. Now I see that it's more like frozen strawberries. I've had to go through hell just to get the strawberries thawed—the screaming and shouting, the hurt feelings and broken promises. It hasn't been easy, but I've got the program and it's helping me to cope.

Sometimes I feel like Dad still doesn't care much about me, Mom tries to smother me, and my brother is only interested in himself. But now I realize we've all been affected by alcoholism and I can only help myself. I can handle things at home most of the time, but if they start to get me down, I get a lot of support from my "new family"—my friends in Alateen.

Things to Think About

Living with alcoholism isn't easy. There are some tough times and I can't always make it through them alone. That's okay. I can call on my Alateen friends and they'll help me find the strength I need.

Tradition One works! Here's how one group used it:

"Our meetings were often silent and dull until the full meaning of the First Tradition sank into our heads. Without group unity, we wouldn't have good meetings and newcomers wouldn't get the help they needed. After reading and studying Tradition One in depth, we all realized we had to give a little bit more of ourselves to make the group work.

"We started to open up and share; then we began to trust each other. This trust made it easier when one of us had a problem and newcomers seemed to feel more at ease, too.

"Today we're thankful for this trust. Our group is together and we know we can lean on each others' shoulders in times of trouble."

Things to Think About

Working together means helping each other. That takes a lot of trust and understanding. Tradition One opens the door. Today I can use it to help make my group strong.

I've always been a smiler, but at one time my smile was not necessarily what I felt on the inside. Smiling covered up a lot of the crying I was doing and it kept people from getting to know the real me.

Now that I'm part of the fellowship, I'm learning to deal with those inside feelings so I can show them as they really are. I don't smile all the time, but when I do, the smile on the outside reflects what's on the inside.

I feel good when I smile. The more I'm around people, the more I realize how contagious that feeling can be. One morning, while I was walking down the street, I started to smile and the results were incredible. People smiled back and some even said, "Good morning." It really helped to get my day off to a great start.

Things to Think About

I don't have to walk around grinning from ear to ear, but a natural smile does a lot more good than a sour look. When I start the day with a smile, it puts me in a positive frame of mind and the result is I feel good all over. And who knows, it might be just the thing somebody else needs to give their day a lift, too.

Sometimes I need to go to more than one meeting a week. But there's only one Alateen group in town and it meets just once a week. What do I do?

No problem. I go to an Al-Anon meeting. I've found one where I'm really comfortable and the people there have made me feel right at home. They give me what I need just when I need it. The more I keep going, the more I realize how grateful I am that Al-Anon and Alateen are part of the same great "family."

Things to Think About

When I'm stuck for a meeting, I try the nearest Al-Anon group. I find just what I'm looking for—friendship, understanding, and good, solid program. It's a big plus for me; I get to add all this to the great things I've gained from Alateen. Together, they make a super combination!

The Twelfth Step is one of my favorites because it wraps up the others. A lot of members have problems with the "spiritual awakening" part of the Step. I did, too. But now I see it as something that makes me more aware of myself and my Higher Power.

Another part says, "we tried to carry this message to others." The best way I can do that is by living the program and setting a good example for others.

When I find myself slipping back into my old ways of thinking, I have to remember to "practice these principles in all my affairs"—at home, at school, at work, and with my friends—not just when I go to my Alateen meetings. I have to take it a day at a time. This helps me to forget those old ways and start fresh each day.

Things to Think About

I'm more alive today than ever before because of the Alateen way of life. To keep on growing, Step Twelve has the answer for me. I have to reach out and lend a hand to other teenagers who need the help of Alateen. And I have to keep working the program in all parts of my life each and every day.

I used to think serenity was life without problems. It's not. It's learning to live *with* anger, arguments, hurt feelings—all the things that make me human.

The program gives me a peace of mind which helps to guide me through my troubles. I have a set of tools to help me tackle my problems, friends who support and understand me, and a Higher Power who loves me. I try to get the most out of life, even the tough spots.

Serenity isn't freedom from the storms of life. It's the calm in the middle of the storm that gets me through. It's up to me to try to keep this calm even when the storm gets worse.

Things to Think About

Serenity isn't something that protects me from hard times. It's a special kind of strength that helps me to face my problems and work through them. Today, when I ask God to grant me serenity, I'll remember that I can "roll with the punches" and make the best of every situation I'm in.

For A.A. members, having a slip means going
back to drinking. Alateens can have slips, too. For
us a slip is a change back to our old attitudes.

When our family, friends, or school get to be too
much for us, do we do what we used to—run away
from our problems or blame them on someone or
something else? Or do we use our program?

Slogans like "How Important Is It?," "Live and
Let Live," and "Let Go and Let God" help us get
over the rough spots. We can turn our attitudes over
to our Higher Power and ask Him to help us get
moving again.

Things to Think About

A slip can trip me up and bring back my old way
of thinking or it can make me work even harder at
using the program. The choice is mine. Today I'll
ask my Higher Power to help me face my problems
honestly so I can get back on the track and grow
some more.

I only existed before coming to Alateen. I just hung around. I took life for granted and often thought it wasn't worth my time and effort to stick around this world.

Then I started going to Alateen. At first I existed on the fellowship and the love I found. It wasn't until I started to look at the Twelve Steps that my life began to have meaning for me.

There are still times when I'm complacent and I turn away from living the program. But when I take a good look at myself and practice the principles of the program in all my affairs, I get involved in life and really start to *live*.

Things to Think About

Life is more than just existing. The program shows me how to live life to the fullest. Today I'll get the most out of living by working the program in everything I do.

People see things differently. Some look at life and see goodness, beauty, friendship, and hope; others look at the same life and see problems, ugliness, loneliness, and despair.

What makes the difference? Attitudes.

In Alateen I've learned that the way I think about a situation determines whether I'll be happy or sad, resentful or understanding, angry or calm, loving or hateful. Working the Steps, Traditions, and slogans helps me develop a happier, more positive attitude and I see more of the good things in my life.

Things to Think About

It's not "things" that make the difference—it's my attitude toward them. The program gives me the tools to be a positive thinker. Using them will help me to look on the bright side of each situation I meet today.

When my father started drinking heavily, my mother tried to stop him, but it got her nowhere. She just ended up sitting on a bar stool drinking right along with him. It seemed as if they were never home when I needed them. I felt lonely and unwanted, as if nobody really cared about me at all.

I started to look for a way out of the rotten life I hated so much. I finally decided that suicide was my only answer. I knew I didn't really want to die; I just wanted somebody to pay some attention to me.

Before I got a chance to try, someone took me to an Alateen meeting and I've been in Alateen ever since. It's helped me understand a lot of things about myself and my parents that I didn't know before. Thoughts about suicide are far from my mind now because I realize I don't have to punish myself to get someone to notice me.

Things to Think About

When my back is against the wall, I want to find a way out. I've found a way—the program. It's like a new beginning and it shows me that life really is worth living.

Before Alateen, self-pity was my master. It almost destroyed me. I tried everything to solve my problems, but nothing worked. I was withdrawn and depressed. I hit bottom and knew I had to do something.

Alateen was my last resort. I'll never forget the warmth and friendship I found at my first meeting. It gave me the boost I needed to keep going.

Now the program has become a way of life. By sharing with the members and trying to apply the program to my life, I'm starting to feel better. The Serenity Prayer has helped me to find acceptance, and Step One continually reminds me that I can control only myself. The slogans are particularly helpful; there's one for every situation in life.

I still have struggles to overcome each day—that's life—but I can see the positive side of them now. I owe that to Alateen. It's showing me the way to a saner, happier, and more productive life.

Things to Think About

When I stop feeling sorry for myself and start working the program, I get a new outlook on life. The obstacles in front of me don't look so big if I use the Steps, the slogans, and the Serenity Prayer to deal with them. Alateen is a new way of life for me and today is my day to start living it.

Everybody has bad days, but I used to get uptight when I had one. I'd spend most of my time cursing my luck and going from one mistake to the next.

Now I try to remember "Easy Does It" and do something I like to do. If I feel like taking a rest, I relax. If I want to talk to someone, I call my Sponsor and we go for a cup of coffee or a soda. If spending the day by myself is what I need, I catch up on some reading, write a few letters, or enjoy one of my hobbies.

I don't have to turn sour when the day does. Slowing down and doing a few things I enjoy helps me get through the day more easily. It can even make a good day out of one that seemed headed for disaster.

Things to Think About

I can't expect myself to feel good all the time. I'm not a robot; I'm a human being. When I have a bad day, I'll try to accept myself where I am, let it go, and relax. Taking time to enjoy myself is a good way to turn the day around.

When I accept the First Step, I know that my life is unmanageable. Now it's time to think about getting help from somewhere. Step Two shows me how to find that help by believing in a Power greater than myself.

A Higher Power works through other people so I don't have to go looking for Him like a needle in a haystack. I just have to keep coming to meetings and sharing with the people there. As I get close to them, I'll be able to tell them about my problems. I'll find out what works for them and start believing that it can work for me, too.

Believing in a Higher Power might not be easy. But it can start when I ask others for help and have the faith that they'll give me a hand with my problems.

Things to Think About

When I go searching for help from a Higher Power, I don't have to look very far. The people in my Alateen group are ready to help me. All I have to do is ask. Getting to know and love them helps me to believe in a Higher Power.

I used to be a lonely person. I didn't think anyone wanted to listen to me so I didn't do much talking.

When I came to Alateen, I found people were willing to listen. So I made up for lost time. I talked and talked and talked. After awhile I stopped talking long enough to realize I wasn't doing much listening. I had an empty feeling inside of me. Without listening, I wasn't learning anything.

Once I began to listen to other people, I started to grow and change. They had a lot to share that really helped me—especially what helped them to solve their problems.

Things to Think About

"Listen and Learn" is a good slogan for talkers like me. Talking is a good way to get my feelings out in the open, but if all I can hear is the sound of my own voice, I'm not going to learn much about handling those feelings. I need to concentrate a little more on the ears and a lot less on the mouth. Listening to my Alateen friends is a great way to learn about helping myself.

Anger is normal. Everyone gets mad at one time or another. But I'm one of those people who used to store up anger. I'd let it build up inside of me until one little thing would set me off and I'd blow up. I found out the hard way that this wasn't very healthy. I was hurting myself and other people by saying and doing things I didn't mean.

My Alateen friends have helped me to work on getting rid of my anger. Sometimes I take a pillow and hit it or I do something physical like bike riding or running. Calling my friends and talking things over helps, too.

Using their ideas has helped me a lot. My insides don't explode like they used to and I'm more relaxed now.

Things to Think About

It's okay to be angry, but how I handle it is what's important. Storing it up can hurt other people as well as myself. Letting it out in healthy ways gives me a chance to calm down and enjoy life.

I was taught that I should love everyone. Hate was something bad. I hated the alcoholic for the drinking and I hated both my parents when they argued. I couldn't control these feelings of hate so I felt I was a bad person.

In Alateen I learned that other people had the same feelings. They helped me to understand that I didn't really hate my parents; I hated what they did. After that I didn't feel so bad.

Now I'm learning how to replace my hate feelings with love and understanding. I know I'm not a bad person after all. I feel good about myself and my parents and there's a lot more love in our home today.

Things to Think About

The program helps me to understand my feelings—even something as strong as hate. I know now that my bad feelings don't make me a bad person. Today I'll concentrate on letting go of those bad feelings and get started on feeling good about myself and the people around me.

When I first came to Alateen, I kept to myself and didn't bother to share my problems with anyone. Actually I didn't want to get close to people, but I turned it around in my head and told myself that they were ignoring me.

So I decided to quit going to meetings and started to look around for people who would accept me and be my friends. The crowd I hung around with drank and did drugs. At first I thought they were cool but I soon felt out of place. Next I tried prayer meetings. The people were friendly enough, but I wasn't comfortable with them, either.

Finally it dawned on me that I'd been looking in the wrong places for acceptance and friendship. Alateen had all that and more waiting for me. I went back to meetings and decided to reach out instead of sitting back. I soon found what I was looking for and it helped me to work out my problems.

Things to Think About

If I'm looking for love and understanding, I don't have to go far. The nearest Alateen group has all that I need and more. It's free for the taking—all I have to do is reach out and accept it.

Removing my shortcomings is like peeling the layers of an onion. First I take off one layer, then another, and another until I get to the center. That's the toughest part.

Peeling an onion isn't easy. Neither is taking the Seventh Step. It says I need to be humble when I ask God to remove my shortcomings. But pride keeps me from reaching the "center." I'm not so sure I really want to change myself that much, even when it means I can be a better person.

But when I look around and see the look in the eyes of my fellow Alateen members, I know this Step works. They keep working at their shortcomings each day, but they don't try to do it themselves; they ask for God's help. They have the serenity that I want. I can have it, too, if I'm willing to let God help me.

Things to Think About

Getting rid of layers and layers of bad feelings isn't an overnight job. But with the help of my Higher Power, it is possible. All I have to do is ask Him. Step Seven gives me the chance to do just that.

For a long time I thought I was to blame for my mother's drinking problem. What a relief it was when she told me my father was to blame. Of course, I believed her. My father wasn't around much because of his job and I was sure my mother felt neglected and that had driven her to drink. I loved my mother and hated what was happening to her. So I made up my mind to punish my father for hurting her and ruining our family. I made fun of him and talked back with all the sarcasm I could think of. In a sick sort of way, I enjoyed watching him suffer.

I didn't know at that time that no one causes alcoholism. It took a lot of listening at meetings before I could really accept this fact and let go of my need to punish my father. Sharing with others affected by alcoholism opened my eyes. I started to realize how much *he* was hurting inside and I tried to stop humiliating him. In time I was able to make amends and concentrate on working with instead of against him in solving our problems.

Things to Think About

It's easy to blame my nonalcoholic parent for everything. That takes the pressure off me. But it's not fair. He has problems, too. Maybe it's time I tried to understand this and give him the support he needs.

Alcoholism is a disease that affects me emotionally, spiritually, and physically. Sometimes I can use it as an excuse. I justify my bad behavior by saying, "I live with an alcoholic." I use the disease as a crutch instead of taking an honest look at myself.

What am I afraid to see? Maybe I don't want to see who I really am. Maybe I'm not ready to change. That would mean giving up alcoholism as an excuse.

I have to stop making excuses if I want to get better. It's not easy, but by looking at myself honestly, I'll be taking a big step toward growing up.

Things to Think About

Living with an alcoholic is a great excuse for my behavior. If I let it, it can keep me from facing the real me. But if I'm honest, I'll realize that I have to do something about *my* life. Today I'll try to stop using alcoholism as a crutch and get on with my own recovery.

I thought love was only a physical thing. But when I got to know some of the people in my Alateen group, I found out that it's actually many different things. It's accepting other people as they are instead of trying to change them; it's being open and honest with each other; it's sharing our deep feelings with one another.

This kind of love draws our group together and makes it strong. The people really care as they reach out to help each other. When newcomers feel this kind of love in our group, it can encourage them to keep coming back. It's a great feeling and I'm glad I'm part of it!

Things to Think About

The love in Alateen is special. It tells me that I'm accepted as I am. It makes me want to share my feelings from the heart and reach out to help other people. It's a strong force in our group and it makes me stronger as a person as well.

To keep things simple is a God-given gift. I used to be able to see things simply, but my reaction to people and things around me covered up a lot of that simplicity in me.

Step Two helped me to find it again. It showed me that part of being "restored to sanity" is learning to "Keep It Simple."

Today when things seem confused and complicated, I try to imagine God holding me in the palm of His hand. It's a simple thought that calms me down and straightens out my thinking. I get a clear idea of what to do and then I get on with doing it as simply as possible.

Things to Think About

Sometimes my thinking gets tied in knots. Alateen shows me a way out. I look at the simple things around me—a smile, a beautiful sunrise, a warm feeling about a friend—and try to "Keep It Simple" in my life today.

Many of us suffer from guilt. We worry about all the bad things we've done and let our feelings eat away at us inside. Sometimes we think we've done more harm than we actually have and we blow things out of proportion. When we allow ourselves to be controlled by our guilt, we get angry at ourselves and strike out at innocent people.

Steps Four and Five can help to relieve us of our guilty feelings. They help us trace the guilt to its real source. Then, in Steps Eight and Nine, we make the amends we need to.

By being honest, we break the grip that guilt has on us. We no longer have to take out our anger on the people around us and we're free from our bad memories of the past.

Things to Think About

When guilt has a hold on me, I make big problems out of little ones and I hurt the people I care about. The program helps me to get to the heart of my guilty feelings. When I face them honestly and make my amends, I'm free to start feeling good again.

Once there was an Alateen group in a city where there were many large A.A. and Al-Anon groups. Unfortunately, Alateen attendance was very poor—only a few people came to the meetings. Some members came only to socialize and not to learn the program of recovery. Others really wanted to have a group, but they weren't willing to take on the responsibility of planning the meetings.

Sometimes someone would come to this group with a problem. That person would stay for a couple of weeks and then stop coming when the problem got better, never feeling responsible to be there to help someone else with a problem. Little by little the group dissolved and disbanded.

If only each member of this group had made an effort to take more responsibility for their individual recovery and for helping each other, the group could have stayed together and grown and these Alateens would have grown up with a better attitude toward life.

Things to Think About

I'm responsible to give and take in our Alateen group. I'm not the most important person. We're all looking for answers and as I get what I need I can help others. Everyone is responsible to build the kind of group where we can trust and love each other. Today it's up to me to do my part.

Our family was falling apart. My father had left and my mother was out parading through bars most of the time. I felt deserted and was ready to run away from it all.

That's when Alateen entered the picture for me. The people loved me and cared for me and helped me get back on my feet. For that reason, I choose them as my new friends.

I know they're not going to run out on me and I don't want to run out on them. I think I'll stick around awhile and try to make the most of things. Maybe someone else will come looking for support and I can be there to help them find the good feeling I've found.

Things to Think About

When things aren't great in my own family, I can look to the fellowship for support. It's like a home away from home to me. It has the love and understanding I've always needed and I can count on it to be there.

I had a hard time respecting my father because he had so many slips. He'd be sober in A.A. for a while; then before long he'd start drinking again. Sometimes he'd accuse me of making him drink. That really hurt. I started to believe what he was saying and I hated him for it. I got to the point where I really didn't care whether he ever made it or not.

Now he's in A.A. again, but I have a different attitude because of the program. I know I'm not to blame for his slips and I'm learning that I don't have to go down with him if he starts to drink again. This kind of detachment has helped me to be more patient and understanding.

Things to Think About

When the alcoholic has a slip, it's hard to respect him if I think he's a failure. But slips are really just the relapses I've heard about in other illness. When I try to understand that, it's a lot easier to let go and practice detachment. Instead of getting tangled up in the alcoholic's struggle for sobriety, I can show him a bit of care and understanding and give some encouragement when it's needed most.

When I went to my first Al-Anon meeting, I was still in Alateen. I felt as though I didn't belong. I didn't say anything because I thought I'd just be wasting time. Soon after, I quit going and went back to my Alateen group.

Then I was asked to speak at an Al-Anon meeting about the transition from Alateen to Al-Anon. One woman said how much she appreciated the insight Alateens could offer to those in Al-Anon. That made me feel good and I decided to go back to the Al-Anon group I'd left.

Since then, I've been getting a lot out of the meetings. I realize now that by listening to Al-Anon members discuss their problems, I may be able to avoid the same ones in my own life. Even if I can't avoid them, at least I'll have the feeling that someone else has been through them, too, and I'll know just where to come to talk about them.

Things to Think About

Al-Anon members tell me they need me. That makes me feel great. The more I attend meetings with them, the more I realize I need them, too. They share their experience, I add my hope, and together we have a special kind of strength.

I was a great one for dragging yesterday into today. I worried about all the mistakes I'd made. It didn't matter that those days were gone forever; I had to hang on to them until I'd made up for all the problems I'd caused. What a mess! My brain was so overloaded with thoughts of the past that I couldn't find a moments' peace to enjoy the present.

That's why it was so good to come to a fellowship that deals in today. With the help of slogans like "One Day at a Time" and "Just For Today," I'm slowly but surely learning that today is a valuable gift. If I can put yesterday behind me and make the most of this day, I know I won't be disappointed.

Things to Think About

Today is a new day. It's a chance to start over. I can forget about yesterday's mistakes; that's all in the past. I can do new things, make new friends, and thank my Higher Power that I'm alive to enjoy today.

I used to hate getting yelled at. It was like a big head with no face, no eyes, no nose—just a huge mouth screaming at me. Sometimes I felt as if I was going to explode, but most of the time I just wanted to crawl into a corner and die.

The program gave me back my self-respect and I can't afford to let anyone take it away from me. Now when someone blows up at me, I work on letting the rage belong to that person and try to keep myself calm. I can do this by touching base with my Sponsor, talking over my feelings about the situation, and letting it go.

Things to Think About

I'm a person and I have a right to be treated like one. Sometimes I allow others to control me, especially when I let their anger get inside me. But if I concentrate on working the program, the calm I feel can stay with *me* and no one will be able to take it away from me.

The alcoholic drinks, and the drinking causes unacceptable behavior. I'm not responsible for that behavior; I'm responsible for me.

That means I don't have to feel guilty when others are trying to blame me for the way they feel or act. If they're fighting, I don't have to fight; if they're screaming and yelling, I don't have to join in. I can try to understand them, but I don't have to feel the way they feel or do what they're doing.

I have a life of my own. With the help of the program, I'm finally free to live it.

Things to Think About

Other people can't make me feel responsible for their lives. I can turn off what I hear, look past what I see, and not let it get to me. I *am* responsible for my own life. I've got a lot of living to do and today's a good day to start.

I'm just starting to realize how great the program is! My life used to be very confused. Now I can turn to the kids in my group for help. I'm learning that I wasn't put in the world to handle everything on my own.

I'm also learning to be more patient. It took me a long time of living a life of anger, hate, fear, and confusion before I finally came to Alateen. Once in awhile I still feel everything has to change overnight, but I stop and realize that if it took me years to reach the point I'm at now, it's going to take more than a day to change.

Things to Think About

Sometimes I have to look beyond myself for help. My Alateen friends are only too willing to give me that help—the kind of help that will keep me growing day by day.

It's very easy for some experienced members of an Alateen group to take control of meetings, influence other members, and monopolize discussions. They think they know it all. They've been around for a while and they feel that gives them the right to speak for the group.

Tradition Two tells us that we can't allow our group to be controlled by members like these. We have to remember that "our leaders are but trusted servants." No one person can act as a conscience of our group. Open and honest discussions among all members at our meetings is the best way to find our Higher Power's true will for our group.

Things to Think About

Some people are leaders, but no one has the right to take over God's territory. The only way an Alateen group can keep going is if *everyone* has the chance to share their feelings and ideas. Tradition Two can make it happen that way in our group if we get to work and apply it.

When I was younger, I was taught that God was watching me, ready to punish me for doing wrong. I learned to be afraid of Him.

In Alateen I found something different. The Steps talked about a Higher Power. To me, a Higher Power was someone who walked in front of me. I wanted God to walk beside me, too, so I started working on a one-to-one relationship with Him.

Today God is more than just my Higher Power; He's a friend that I can talk to. I feel good with Him and I know I don't have to be afraid of Him anymore.

Things to Think About

Thanks to the program I have a very special friend: Someone who loves and understands me and doesn't get mad because I'm not perfect; Someone who knows when I'm up or down; Someone I can talk to and love. I call that Someone "God" and He's the greatest friend I have.

Alateen is more than just my group; it's a fellowship that reaches out to the whole world. There are groups everywhere that are trying to follow the same ideas as the group to which I belong.

It's easy to forget that I have a responsibility to those groups. Sometimes I get wrapped up in my own little world and forget that we're all part of each other in Alateen. Each of us is responsible to help keep Alateen alive and well throughout the world so that more people can be helped.

I can live up to that responsibility by trying to live the program to the best of my ability each day and doing my part to make my group stronger. Another way is taking part in service work. That helps me reach beyond myself and my group and get involved with Alateen worldwide. It's a great way to grow personally and it's *my* way of helping to strengthen our links as a fellowship.

Things to Think About

When I become involved in service work, I see that there are thousands of groups and kids all around the world who are trying to work the same program as I am. If we all try to help each other we'll be a lot stronger. I need Alateen and Alateen needs me; "Together We Can Make It" a better world today.

Somebody criticized me, I'm angry. Should I be? I won't know until I take some time to really think about what's been said.

Is the criticism justified? If it is, I'd better accept it and do something about changing myself. If it isn't, I can let go of it and stop worrying about it right now.

Things to Think About

Criticism can really get to me unless I think it through. If it's false, I don't need to waste my energy getting all upset. It's true, I can take it to heart and use my program to help change things for the better.

For a long time after I came to Alateen, I sat back and watched other people get involved. I thought that if *I* got involved, my personal recovery program would fly out the window.

I was wrong. I know now that I hurt myself by not giving a little more time and effort to this program.

When I did get involved, I found it actually helped me with my program. I started to give back a small part of what I was getting by sharing my feelings at meetings, listening to other members, and taking on jobs in the group. And I found that I was getting a lot more than I could ever give.

Things to Think About

People say that you get back from the program what you put into it. How true it is! When I give back what I can—even if it's just a small amount—I get more out of Alateen. By trying to help others, I help myself, too.

Sometimes I feel trapped by the events in my life. I feel helpless and unable to change my situation.

That's when I have to think about choices. I need to remember that while I'm powerless to change other people, I can always choose my own attitude toward an unpleasant situation.

The program gives me the chance to make some good choices: reading Al-Anon/Alateen literature, practicing the Twelve Steps, working on myself, and a lot more. It's up to me whether or not I use them, but I have to remember that my reactions are always the results of the choices I make.

Things to Think About

When I believe that someone or something else is in control of my attitude, let me remember that I'm always free to choose my reactions. The program helps me gain the freedom to make wise choices that are good for me. I choose to put that freedom to work in my life today.

How willing am I to study and apply the program to my life? Do I just talk about it because it sounds good? Or do I really use it? Do I use it to make myself look good in front of everyone else? Or do I use it to help me grow?

If I'm not willing to grow along spiritual lines, then I can't say that I'm applying Alateen ideas. Being a part of Alateen comes from living the Twelve Steps. I have to dig a little deeper and be willing to work the program the best way I know how.

All I'm asked to be is *willing.* As I become more and more willing, I give myself a chance to grow.

Things to Think About

Willingness is the key which opens the door to a new life for me. If I'm *willing* to make the program a part of me, good things can happen. I'll solve some of the trouble spots in my life and I'll start to grow a little bit every day.

I went to Alateen because my mother wanted me to go. I was convinced I didn't have any problems. When my mother asked me if I liked the meetings, I said "Yes" to keep her happy, but in my heart I hated them. I stayed for a few weeks. Then, when things started getting worse at home and school, I said the program wasn't working for me and stopped going to meetings. I was sure that I could take care of things on my own.

I couldn't. I felt as if I was alone against the world. But I was too proud to go back to Alateen and ask for help. I came very close to having a nervous breakdown. My mother suggested I try Alateen again. I didn't want to go back because I was scared what people would think of me. But finally I put my pride aside and went.

This time I went for *me* and felt the love I desperately needed. I can share my feelings and problems with other people instead of trying to handle everything by myself.

Things to Think About

Pride can make me walk away from the fellowship. It keeps me from getting the help I need when the going gets tough. When I can put my pride behind me, I'll find a group of people ready to help me work the program.

All of us want to be respected, including the alcoholic. But it's not easy respecting someone who seems to be destroying his own life as well as ours.

I've come to believe that the reason it was so hard to respect other people in my life was because I didn't respect myself. I felt lousy inside and the way I was acting made it hard for anyone to like me, including myself.

Alateen has helped me to appreciate who I am and have confidence in what I say and do. As I go through the Steps and use the Traditions, I gain more respect for myself and it seems a bit easier to understand and respect the people around me, even the alcoholic.

Things to Think About

Respect is a two-way street. If I want people to respect me, I have to be willing to respect them. But how can I expect that to happen if I don't respect myself. I'm learning to feel a lot better about myself in Alateen and as that good feeling grows in me, it has a way of reaching out to others. Today I believe in myself and can give other people the kind of respect that I'd like to have from them.

I always thought alcoholics were skid-row bums. I knew my parents drank a lot, but we had lots of money so I was sure they couldn't possibly have a drinking problem. As things became worse, I started to feel angry and resentful. But on the outside, I pretended that everything was fine. I was too proud to admit that my life was falling apart. When someone suggested that I go to Alateen, I told her I wasn't one of *those* kinds of people.

I kept pretending for a long time—so long that my mother and father nearly died of alcoholism. I guess that's what finally woke me up. I came to the fellowship and the kids in Alateen set me straight. They told me to stop playing my "poor little rich kid" routine and face facts—my parents have a disease called alcoholism. It can strike any family—even mine. When I accepted this, I let go of my "stuck-up" attitude and let other people show me the way to get help for myself.

Things to Think About

Alcoholism is a *real* illness. It affects *real* people from all walks of life, and it causes *real* pain. I'd like to close my eyes and pretend it doesn't exist, but it does. The sooner I stop pretending and admit that it's part of my life, the sooner I'll be able to accept the help I need to get better.

When I was younger, I felt very lonely and unwanted. I tried to get people to like me by impressing them with my schoolwork. I thought if they saw my good grades, they'd think I was something special and they'd pay more attention to me. It didn't work. In fact, it made me feel more alone. I won a lot of prizes because of my good grades, but I always felt I'd failed because prizes weren't what I wanted. I needed to know that people loved *me* and care about *me.*

Now I realize I was so busy trying to be perfect that I turned people away; nobody could have reached me at that time. Since coming to Alateen, I've learned to relax my standards a bit. I still get high marks, but I'm through with putting on a show for other people. I try to accept myself as I am, without any of the "frills," and that's making it easier to be natural with others. I'm not lonely anymore because I know there are a lot of people who really do care about me just the way I am.

Things to Think About

When I'm feeling alone, sometimes I forget just how good a person I really am. I think I have to do and say things to make people like me. I don't. I just have to be myself. With the program showing me how to use "Easy Does It," I can be my best self today without having to be perfect.

For many years I tried to change my family, telling everyone what to do and how to do it. If they didn't change, I'd get upset and loose my temper.

In Alateen I realized that I couldn't change them; I couldn't control anybody's behavior. I learned that *I* was the only person *I* could change.

With the help of the other members, I started to look at my good and bad points. Little by little I worked on getting rid of the bad ones and making the good ones better. Today I feel a lot better concentrating on changing myself instead of everybody else.

Things to Think About

Alateen gives me the chance to change myself. As I take my mind off changing the people around me and start working on myself, I'll be a lot happier. Today, when I ask for "Courage to change the things I can," I'll remember that the only thing I *can* change is me.

Before I came to Alateen, I didn't know how to handle all the situations that came up in our family. We were all affected by the disease of alcoholism. I had a lot of resentment and hatred toward my dad, but I thought my mom was the bad one so I blamed her for most of the things that happened. I had so many bad feelings that I couldn't live with myself.

That's when I came to Alateen. The people helped me to understand why my dad did the things he did and why I reacted the way I did. I started to understand my mom a lot better and I realize now that she was only trying to keep our family together.

Today my Alateen friends give me a lot of suggestions about how to use the program to handle my problems. With their help, I feel a lot better about my family.

Things to Think About

Sometimes I forget that I'm not the only one in the family who has problems. Alateen helps me to remember that alcoholism is a family disease. We're all affected by it. I can help a lot today by trying to understand and care about my family and by doing my best to live the program.

We're not perfect. We can't solve all our problems alone. A Higher Power can make things easier for us. But He won't just take over our lives and let us sit back and do nothing. We have to decide to let go and let Him help us. That's where Step Three can help.

Turning our will over to the care of a Higher Power is an important part of our program. It helps us to break away from the past with a new sense of direction. We stop controlling people and situations in our lives. Our good feelings come back and we find peace of mind working the program.

Things to Think About

I find real comfort knowing there's a Power greater than myself who can keep me going in the right direction. Alateen shows me how to let go and let that Power work.

I used to enjoy criticizing other people. When they did things that bothered me, it felt good to get back at them by telling them what was wrong with them. It made me feel big and important.

Now that I'm in Alateen I realize that I don't have to put down other people to make myself feel better. My job is to take my own inventory. I have to fix what's wrong with me, not what I think is wrong with others. I don't have the right to criticize the alcoholic, the nonalcoholic, or any other person. I'm not responsible for their lives and they can do without my nagging.

Now when people criticize me, I know what I made them feel like. Instead of resenting the criticism, I look at what's been said, try to learn something from it, and apply what I can to my life.

Things to Think About

Other people can take care of themselves; they don't need me to point out their faults. Instead of criticizing others to make myself feel good, I'll get busy with my own inventory. If I look at myself today, I may find more good there than I expected.

In Step Four I took a look at my problems. In Step Five I admitted them. Now, in Step Six, I have to ask myself, "What am I going to do about them?" I have a good idea about what's wrong with me and I want to change those things right now.

Maybe it's time to sit down and think about where I'm going. That will help me sort out what needs to be changed right away and what I can take care of a little later. Then, when I want to move ahead, I can, knowing that I'm entirely ready to have my defects removed.

Things to Think About

It's not good to rush my way through the Twelve Steps. Step Six is a good place to stop and think. I've come a long way and I know myself better now than ever before. But I still have a long way to go. By rushing into it, I might wander off in the wrong direction. Being *entirely* ready before I get moving again will give me a better understanding of what I really want.

I didn't care much about having friends unless I could get something from them. If they had money, I hung around with them. If they had good contacts, I got to know them so I could get in with the crowd. I did things that hurt some of them deeply, but it didn't matter if it meant getting the best deal possible.

When I came to Alateen, I found people who knew the real meaning of friendship. They cared about me, even though I'd never done anything for them. By their example they showed me how important people could be to me—not in the way I used to think, but as close and trusted friends. I learned from these people that friendship is a give-and-take thing. I'd done a lot of taking; now it was time to start giving. When I began to put more into my relationships with people, I felt better. I found the courage to make amends for my past and started to show my new friends how much I really cared about them.

Things to Think About

Real friendship isn't some cheap thing I can take for granted. It's something I need to make me feel like a whole person. In the fellowship I've found good friends who really value me. When I think about how much they've done for me, it makes me want to give a little of myself to show them how much they mean in my life.

I was very close to my brother. When I found out he had a drinking problem, I was shattered. I felt sorry for him and wanted to protect him. When my parents asked him to leave home, I told them what I thought of them and swore I'd leave too, as soon as I could arrange to move in with him.

But my brother disappeared for several weeks and my plans went out the window. The next time I saw him, he told me that he was going to A.A. and mentioned that Alateen might be good for me. I was ready to do anything to help him, so I went the next night.

At first I was angry when they told me there was nothing I could do to help him. I was soon to realize that a change in my attitude could help a lot. I stopped trying to protect and feel sorry for him. I was a lot more comfortable with that and I think he was, too. As for my parents, I've given up my grudge against them because I realize they only did what they thought was right.

Things to Think About

Because I love the alcoholic, I want to protect him from getting hurt. But at the same time, I may be keeping him from getting the help he needs. When I accept the truth about alcoholism, I can do the one thing that really *can* help: love him and let go.

I used to think everyone in the group looked up to me. Since I'd been in the group the longest, I thought they expected me to talk and keep the meetings going. So that's what I did. There were times when I wanted to just sit and listen, but I put those feelings aside so I could carry out my responsibility to the group.

Then one night another member said she never got enough time to talk because I was always commenting on everything. I was really hurt and stayed away from meetings for several weeks with an "I'll show them" attitude. But while I was away, I realized something important: It's not my responsibility to run the meetings.

Now I *can* sit and listen if I want to because I know I'm a member, not a supervisor. I feel a lot more comfortable and I think the group does, too.

Things to Think About

Meetings are a time for sharing. When everyone takes part, everyone benefits. If I'm taking up a lot of time talking, I may be hurting others in the group, not to mention myself. Maybe it's time I opened my ears instead of my mouth; I might learn a thing or two by listening to someone besides myself!

Would I go to another country and expect people to understand my language? I make about as much sense to the alcoholic when he's drinking. I can't speak his language and he can't speak mine.

It's frustrating. I've tried reasoning with him, yelling at him, crying, and running away. Nothing seems to get through.

When I let God act as the interpreter between us, things are a lot better. Instead of reacting to his arguments and becoming angry myself, I try to keep quiet and get a hold on my temper. It helps me stay calm so I can choose the best times to communicate with the alcoholic and show some of the real feelings I have for him.

Things to Think About

Trying to reach the alcoholic when he's drinking is a good way to get myself upset. It seems as if he doesn't want to listen to what I'm saying. Using "Let Go and Let God" helps me deal with my frustration. I see that there are times when the alcoholic *can't* understand me. Accepting that helps me to be patient and wait for the right time to try and talk to him.

We all come to Alateen because someone close to us has a drinking problem. That's important. We know that we share our inner thoughts and feelings with others who understand.

Alateen is people helping each other to get better. When we work together on a problem, sharing our experiences, strength, and hope, we help each other. It's the cement that holds us together.

If our group got involved with other organizations, that special feeling would be lost. We wouldn't have the time or energy to help each other. Could we really afford that, knowing how important Alateen is to all of us?

Things to Think About

The Third Tradition is our common bond. It's being accepted, not rejected. It's knowing that I'm not alone, that other people my age have lived through the same things I have. It's a tremendous sense of belonging. I don't want anything to take those feelings away.

What do we need for a healthy life? Food, rest, and exercise. These are physical needs. They always seem to be on our minds, especially when we don't take care of them.

But we have other needs, too. We need to be loved and cared for, we need to feel appreciated, and we need to know we're doing something useful with our lives. These are spiritual needs. Sometimes we're not even aware of them; sometimes we just ignore them because our physical needs seem to be more important.

The program gives us a chance to do something about our spiritual needs. We find people who really care about us and make us feel special. We come to believe in a Higher Power who loves us. We start to use the program and find that our lives have a real purpose.

Things to Think About
Alateen is a spiritual program that gets to the heart of what I need. When I look after my spiritual needs, all other things in my life have a way of taking care of themselves. I want to be healthy, inside and out, and I'll put the program into practice today.

When alcoholism took over our family, most of us asked, "Why me?" Some of us withdrew. We made excuses for not going out or having people in. We thought we had to stay around to referee the fights between our parents. But that only gave us more time to feel miserable and lonely.

Some of us couldn't get out of the house fast enough. Every time there was trouble, we took off and stayed away for a long time. It was our way of dealing with what was going on at home.

Running away and withdrawing only hurts us. With the help of the program and the new friends we make, we start to face the fact that we live with an alcoholic. But that doesn't have to control our lives.

We may not be able to change our home situation, but we can change ourselves and our attitude toward it. And that's a good beginning.

Things to Think About

Running away and withdrawing from my problems never helps me to face the truth. I live with an alcoholic; that much I can't change. But if I work the program today—the Steps, Traditions, and slogans—I can start to change *myself* and I won't have to run away from the truth anymore.

There have been times when I've felt like giving up, but thanks to God and my Alateen friends, I didn't. They gave me the strength to move forward instead of backward.

I doubted the program for a long time. But by going to meetings, talking things over with other members, and trying to live "One Day at a Time," it gradually got through to me.

Today I'm happy. I have the strength and courage to move on and I know that wherever I go, I'm never alone. My friends have shown me the way to let go of my doubts and start believing in me.

Things to Think About

Doubt is a quitter's word. I'm here to do my best, to keep trying to move ahead. The program has shown me the way to do just that. It's given me the courage to be the kind of person I am today.

I spent my first few Alateen meetings with my eyes glued to the floor. I felt like a real nothing. I didn't talk. I just came in, sat down, listened, and left as soon as the meeting was over. People tried to reach out to me, but I wouldn't let them.

Then one night I heard someone telling my story. I looked up and realized the girl was a friend from my childhood. When the meeting was over, I hung around and finally found the courage to talk to her. It felt good to renew the friendship, but I felt as if there was something more between us. That's when I asked her to be my personal Sponsor and she said she'd be glad to.

Since that night I've changed. I'm comfortable with her because she gives me the freedom to be me. She laughs *with* me, and she lets me cry when I need to get the pain out. She shares her ups and downs, too. She's honest and doesn't let me depend on her for my answers. Instead, she shows me how the program can give me all the answers I need.

Things to Think About

My Sponsor is a special person in my life. She gives me care and love and a lot of straight talk, the kind I need. But most important of all, she shares the program with me. It's given her the answers when she's needed them, and I know she hopes it will have the answers for me, too.

There's beauty in the rain. It refreshes some flowers—they come back stronger than ever—while others die to allow new and better ones to grow. Plants grow taller and greener; some are given a new strength when old dirt is washed away. The rain brings out the real beauty that's around us.

Alateen is like the rain. It refreshes me. I used to feel dirty; I was dishonest with myself and others. I wore a mask that said, "Everything is fine here," when it wasn't that great at all.

With the help of the program, my old mask and fears were washed away and I've come back strong. My old defects have started to die away, making places for new and better qualities. Just as the rain strengthens new plants and helps them to grow, the program gives me the chance to be a stronger and growing person.

Things to Think About

We start as seeds. With the care we get in Alateen, we sprout. Our stems grow high and thick; our roots, deep and strong. Our branches reach out. Then we bud and, with the help of the program, we grow again.

I'm grateful for the adults who care enough to spend their time and energy sponsoring Alateen. The Sponsors in my group helped me when I was having a hard time accepting my parents. I resented my alcoholic mother because of what she'd taken from our family, and I hated my father because I felt he could have given me more than he did.

Our Alateen Group Sponsors didn't try to act like parents to me; they didn't even try to defend my parents. They simply accepted what I had to say with understanding. Then they introduced me to a few other members of Al-Anon and A.A. When I listened to these people, I realized how my parents felt. In time, I met some Alateens who had no parents at all, and it occurred to me that I had a lot to be grateful for after all.

Today I realize my parents have lots of love inside of them. Although they don't always know how to show it, I know they're trying to do their best and that's fine with me.

Things to Think About

I expect a lot from my parents, sometimes so much that I forget about their feelings. Lots of kids I know would give anything for the chance to live with both parents. I'll try to remember that today and work on being a little more grateful for all they do for me.

I'm in Alateen to work on changing myself. I'd like to get rid of all my defects of character right now, but I know if I try to do everything at once, I won't get anywhere.

Instead I'll try "First Things First." I'll take my time and decide what's important. What do I need to work on first? When I've decided, I'll start with that. If there's something I can do about it today, I'll do it.

There's a lot of me to change. When I work on one thing at a time, taking step by step, it makes the path to recovery a lot easier to walk.

Things to Think About
When I look at all my faults at the same time, it's too much for me to handle. "First Things First" helps me to work on my problem areas one at a time, concentrating on the important ones first. My defects stop getting me down and I can start working on being a whole person again.

I thought I was the center of the universe. I wanted everybody to feel sorry for me because of my terrible childhood. I thought my family should feel remorse because of the way they treated me. Everyone was supposed to do things my way and live up to my standards. At the same time, I thought I shouldn't have to do anything I didn't want to do, regardless of who wanted me to do it.

Now that I'm in the program, I have a different attitude. I think I've grown up a little bit. I realize that the world wasn't created just for me, that people aren't here just for my benefit. I'm starting to understand that my father has an illness and that he doesn't want to be the way he is. I can't blame him, or other people, for the way I am. I have to stand on my own feet and face each day the best I can.

Things to Think About

I used to think the world revolved around me. Now I'm glad it doesn't. I'm just a part of it, but because of the program, I can make it a good part. If I take care of my corner of the world and let others look after theirs, everybody, including me, will be a lot better off today!

Some time ago a boy came to our meeting. He was a lot younger than the rest of us, but I could tell he was in rough shape by the look in his eyes. He didn't have much to say at the meeting, but when he did speak, the pain in his voice matched the look on his face.

When the meeting was over, I wanted to make arrangements to call him during the week. But he seemed to be in a hurry and he was out the door before I could talk to him. I took it for granted he'd be back the following week. He wasn't, and to this day, no one knows who he was or where he came from. I think about him a lot. At times I even worry about him because I saw some of myself in him. I've shared my feelings with my group and they've helped me put them in perspective. All I can do is turn this boy over to my Higher Power and hope he's found someone who can help him to stop hurting.

Things to Think About

There's no age limit on pain. That's why the program works. But not everyone can accept its help. Because the program means so much to me, I used to hurt a little each time when someone left and never came back. Now I realize I just have to keep reaching out to those who come and hope they'll stay long enough to find some relief for their pain.

Pride kept me from getting to Alateen a lot sooner than I did. I wanted everybody to think I was perfect. I didn't want them to know that I wasn't able to handle my problems by myself.

When I finally came to Alateen, I started to be more honest with myself and others. The program helped me to admit that I do have problems and I learned to accept other people's help in dealing with them.

My pride can still be a problem today. If I'm not careful, it will give me a perfect excuse for procrastinating. But if I try to keep it in check, I can help others to overcome their pride, too, so they won't have to wait around as long as I did to get all the good things the program has to give.

Things to Think About

Pride gets me into a lot of trouble. It tells me that I'm better than I really am and it keeps me from asking for the help I need. The program has a good way to help me get rid of it—by being *honest* as I reach out to others and let others reach out to me.

I had problems and bad feelings long after the alcoholic left our home. Changing my attitude didn't happen overnight; it took time. I'm still working on it today.

I have to remember that alcoholism is an illness. I don't have the power to make any alcoholic start or stop drinking. I'm only responsible for me.

I can't blame the alcoholic anymore and make excuses for my poor behavior. I have to look at myself and use the program to become the person I want to be.

Things to Think About

It's easy to think that when the alcoholic is gone, my life will run smoothly. Not true! I still have lots of problems to work out. With the help of the program, I'll stop blaming the alcoholic and start doing something about me today.

Sometimes I reject people's attempts to be nice to me. I find it hard to accept a compliment and feel uncomfortable when someone tries to do me a favor. I don't think I deserve it.

That's when I need to remind myself that it's okay to accept the good things others have to offer. Maybe they see something in me I can't see in myself.

I'm worth a lot more than I'm willing to give myself credit for. Taking a closer look at myself, with the help of the program, can help me start to believe in myself as much as other people do.

Things to Think About

Other people keep telling me I'm a worthwhile person. Maybe it's time I started to believe them. Working hard at the program will give me a positive feeling that will help *me* see the good in myself, too.

When I go fishing, I have to bait the hook in order to catch a fish. I don't always get one, but as long as I get a nibble, I keep rebaiting the hook. When I don't, I pack up and go home.

Since coming to Alateen and finding out about alcoholism and its effect on the family, I realize I often feel like the fish and I'm learning not to take the alcoholic's "bait." Whenever I'm tempted to, I say, "Easy Does It," remembering if I open my mouth to bite, there's a jagged hook hidden under the juicy bait. Then I ask myself, "How Important Is It?"

If I swim past the bait, I can get a clearer picture of the man at the end of the line. He doesn't seem like such a monster after all. Instead he looks sick. If I dodge the bait, the man often packs up and leaves me alone. Even if he stays, I feel safe knowing I've been good to myself by keeping myself off his hook each day.

Things to Think About

The alcoholic wants me to swallow his ideas "hook, line, and sinker." With the help of the program, I don't have to get caught anymore. Instead I can try to understand that he's sick, let go of the line he's feeding me, and enjoy the freedom I have today.

I used to plan things for two or three weeks ahead and worry about whether or not they'd turn out right. I was always confused because I had so many things to think about all at once.

Now I'm learning to slow down and take life "One Day at a Time." Of course I have to think about my future and what I want to do and be. But I don't have to live in tomorrow and worry about things out of my control.

Today has only twenty-four hours. I can put them to good use if I let the program lead the way. I can help somebody with a problem, take my own inventory, or work on an important part of the program for me. This will help get my mind off the future and back on today where it belongs.

Things to Think About

What's down the road for me? I'm not sure, but now I know I don't have to be afraid to face it. Today is the day that counts, and thanks to the program, I have a great way to make the most of it.

As I grow in the program, I realize more and more that helping others helps me. Phoning newcomers, sharing my thoughts and feelings, and participating in the group makes me feel good about myself.

One way of "carrying the message" is speaking on a panel at public meetings. It gives me the chance to help someone who may never have heard about Alateen. But more than that, it helps me see what the program means to me and that gives *me* a real boost.

Things to Think About

Doing Twelfth Step work is good for me. It's a great opportunity to think about all the program has done for me and to put it into practice by carrying the message to others. When I give the program away, it has a special way of staying with me and helping me to grow.

One morning, as I was walking, I spotted a puddle, shining and smooth. It was simple and beautiful. Then I ran through it, making it dark and muddled.

I realize now how our lives are like that. We all have puddles of feeling inside of us. They'll stay clear and shining if we don't let others upset us. But they'll grow dark and murky if we start to let people control our lives.

Alateen shows me that I have a choice. I can keep my puddles clear and serene or I can allow others to muddle my puddles. It's up to me.

Things to Think About

I'm in charge of me. Do I want other people to take away my good feelings about today? Alateen gives me the right to make that choice for myself.

I decided to go to Alateen on my own. At first I was scared, but when the members started sharing, I found out they had the same problems I had. For awhile, I had a hard time understanding everyone. I think I wanted to be the only one in the world with problems, yet at the same time I wanted help.

They encouraged me to keep going to meetings and I did. Gradually I began to understand myself and my family. The more I understood, the better I was able to help myself.

Working the Twelve Steps opened doors for me. I found a new kind of love for my parents and myself. I stayed out of trouble and started getting good grades in school.

The program seems like a miracle to me—only because I want it to work. I have the will to do what I want and I know that I want to keep coming back.

Things to Think About

When I really want what the program has to offer, I'll do anything to get it. Going to meetings, sharing my problems with others, working the Steps; all these are part of the new way of life I call Alateen. It's mine today if I'm willing to work for it.

I haven't had much experience with seeing someone drunk. Although my father is an alcoholic, he's been sober since I was very young. I can only remember a few times when I actually saw him drinking.

But that doesn't mean I can't get something out of Alateen. The program is a great help in other parts of my life besides alcoholism. It helps me to think of my Higher Power as someone who can help me instead of someone I have to obey all the time. It's a big help in getting me through rough days and bad moods.

The fact that my dad still goes to A.A. is an inspiration to me. It makes me want to understand more about him and his alcoholism. But more than that, it makes me want to keep working my own program for me.

Things to Think About

Alateen helps me understand alcoholism. But it doesn't stop there. It's a program of living that can help me understand myself and gives a sense of direction to every part of my life.

I know there's more to life than my problems, but sometimes it's hard to remember that. When I start thinking about what the alcoholic is doing, I forget about what I can do to put my own life in order.

That's why I'm in Alateen. Step One helps me to let go of the alcoholic's problem and starts me working on my own. The rest of the Steps show me how to shrink my problems down to a manageable size so I can get some enjoyment out of life.

Sometimes things are still hard to handle and my problems seem too much for me. But now I know that the problems I have to face aren't nearly as big as the Power behind me.

Things to Think About

Sometimes my mind takes a detour and I spend a lot of time thinking about problems that aren't my concern. Today I'll use the program to let go of those problems so they can't take away the good times I want to enjoy. The Twelve Steps help to keep me on the right track—solving my own problems.

When we live with alcoholism, we often take out our anger on those closest to us. We're afraid to show the alcoholic our feelings so we strike out at other family members. Sometimes, when we're really upset, we may even hit them. We know we're being unfair and that makes us feel guilty, but we can't seem to stop. Eventually we turn the anger on ourselves.

By sharing at meetings we learn that we're not alone in feeling angry. Other people have felt the same way and have even done the same things we have. We also learn that anger is a feeling—*it* isn't wrong; we just have to change the way we show it so we don't hurt ourselves or others.

Today I'm starting to let out my angry feelings in positive ways. I've stopped picking on my family and I feel a lot better, too.

Things to Think About

Anger has a way of bringing out the worst in me unless I deal with it. Alateen shows me how to be honest about my angry feelings, which helps me channel my feelings into something constructive. I'm a lot happier today and so are the people around me!

When it's raining or foggy, it seems as if the sun has gone away. But I know it's only hidden by the clouds. I have faith that the sun is always there.

Because of alcoholism in my home, sometimes it feels as if love has disappeared. I search hard to find it, but I can't see it. It's clouded over by my bad feelings.

When that happens, I have to try hard to believe that love, just like the sun, is always there. It's not easy to have that kind of faith, but the program gives me Step Two as a beginning.

Things to Think About

Alateen has helped me to have faith in things I can't see. I found a Higher Power in Step Two. When I believe in that Power, I can believe in love.

The people who attend Alateen meetings share two common problems: an alcoholic in their lives and a lot of pain.

The great thing about the fellowship is that we can identify with each other. We understand what it's like to live with an alcoholic and somehow the pain isn't as hard to deal with when somebody else knows how we feel.

Sharing the pain is a beginning for me. It's a way of getting all my negative feelings out in the open. After awhile, when I start to grow in the program, I'll be able to share more positive things.

Things to Think About

Everyone in Alateen knows what it's like to hurt. That makes it a lot easier to share the pain that's inside of me. Talking about my problems is a good place to start today. In time, I'll be sharing lots of good feelings, too.

When I first came to Alateen, I put on an act because I was shy and lacked self-confidence. I soon learned that everyone in the program is equal. I wanted to feel better so I started to look at myself.

The Fourth Step helped change my life. At first I did a lot of analyzing and that didn't work. Aiming for perfection wasn't the way to go either. So I kept it simple: I looked at the good side first and then worked on one thing at a time on the bad side. It made me realize that I have a lot of good qualities that I've missed because I've been spending a lot of time concentrating on my faults.

Things to Think About

I'm a lot happier today because I'm working at being a better person. Taking my own inventory helps me to know who I am and what I can do. I'm more honest with myself and I'm learning to see all the good that's inside of me instead of just the bad.

After I've taken my inventory, I want to change myself in many ways. Sometimes I grow impatient. I want to make up for lost time and I try to change too much too fast. I often become discouraged and end up saying, "What's the use?"

That's where "Easy Does It" can help. It slows me down and gives me a more realistic view of what I need to do. I can't change myself overnight, but when I take my time, I can keep coming until I find a pace that's just right for me.

Things to Think About

It takes time for a seed to grow into a tree. Changing myself takes time, too. When I want those changes to happen NOW, I'll try to relax, use "Easy Does It," and be more patient with myself.

Before I came to Alateen, I had a hard time controlling my temper. I used to blame myself and my mother for my dad's drinking problem. I talked back to her and when things really got out of control, I even hit her.

Reading literature, using the slogans and the Serenity Prayer, and practicing the Twelve Steps and Traditions helped me to calm down and understand more about alcoholism and myself. Now I realize it's not my fault that my father has a drinking problem. I've stopped blaming my mom, too. My temper did a lot of damage to our relationship so now I've started to make amends to her. The greatest amend I can make is simply working the program for myself.

Things to Think About
Sometimes I let my temper get control of me. The program shows me how to reverse the situation. When I take it easy and keep my temper under control, I learn more about myself and my relationships with other people are a lot better.

Prayer is asking our Higher Power for guidance and direction in our lives. Meditation is listening for a reply. But how do we know when we've heard the answer?

Practicing the Eleventh Step keeps us in "conscious contact" with our Higher Power. Keeping the lines of communication open helps us to recognize the "signposts" and some things seem to fall into place.

The answers we get may not be what we want to hear. They may be hard to accept. But we have to have faith that our Higher Power is there to help us.

Things to Think About

People say that God answers prayers in three ways: yes, no, or wait. Alateen helps me to listen for His answers to *my* prayers and to accept whatever these answers are. Today I'll try to listen to my Higher Power so I can get to know what He has in mind for me.

Sometimes it's hard to find people I can trust. I want to tell them about my feelings, but I'm afraid they'll spread it all over. That's why anonymity is so important.

At my meetings I have the chance to express what's inside me. I don't have to feel that I'm in another world, alone in silence, with no one to turn to. Anonymity gives me the confidence to speak up knowing that nobody is going to gossip about what I've said. It's that special kind of "glue" that binds us together in trust.

Things to Think About

Anonymity brings out the best in me. It gives me a chance to be open and honest with others because I know that no one is going to talk about me or what I've said. It protects me and opens up a whole new world of friendship and trust.

My parents tried to buy my love and affection. I guess each of them thought if they "paid" me enough, I'd take sides with them during our family fights. At times I enjoyed it because I used to play one against the other and came out the winner every time. But in the end, I felt really guilty about doing this.

In Alateen I learned I could get rid of my guilt and help my parents by changing my attitude. Instead of letting them "buy me off," I tried to talk to them about how I felt. I stopped taking sides and started to show them a little gratitude for the good things they did for me.

Now I'm free of the guilt I once had about our relationship. And I think they are, too. We can relate to each other as people now. My parents know I have a special kind of love for them and I know they love me in a very real way, too.

Things to Think About

When I was caught in the middle between my parents, I thought love was cheap. Now I know it can't be bought. I want to love my parents and I want them to love me. Being honest about *my* feelings can help. Today I'll get out of the middle by showing my parents the real love I have for them.

Sometimes I'm so mixed up with self-pity that I blame those around me for my problems. Looking honestly at myself makes it clear that many problems start with me.

Solving these problems starts with me, too. If I can take one problem that's bothering me and quietly think about it, asking myself how I could have handled it differently, I might find an answer to my trouble. Have I read a piece of literature or thought about talking to others in the fellowship?

It isn't easy to take responsibility for my own actions, but when I do, I stop feeling sorry for myself and get on with working out my difficulties. It all begins with me.

Things to Think About
If there's a problem in my life and I caused it, that's tough to face. But it's honest. That helps me work on solving it with the help of the program.

Newcomer: "I know if my mother would just stop drinking, everything would be great and we could get back to some normal living again."

Member: "That's what I thought, too. I expected life to be a bowl of cherries. What a dreamer! I'm really thankful my father is sober, but getting rid of the booze was just the beginning. I guess I was counting on his sobriety to solve all my problems. It didn't. *I* still have to look after *my* life. And that's why I keep coming back to Alateen."

Things to Think About

My life doesn't depend on whether the alcoholic is drinking or sober. I'm here to work on me. The program has the answers to *my* problems and gives me courage to work them out for myself.

Traditions—who needs them? WE DO—to keep our group together. The strength of our Alateen group depends upon how well we try to practice the Traditions.

When we don't pay enough attention to them, we hurt ourselves and our group. We ignore something that could give everybody a chance to grow.

But when we take the Traditions seriously, we find they're more interesting than we thought. And as we learn more about them, we start to see that they're another great way to share our experience, strength, and hope.

Things to Think About

I'll do my best today to learn more about the Traditions. They're the result of lessons learned the hard way. Maybe if we all do our part, we won't have to make the same mistakes and our group will be able to give everyone the help they need.

I'm a special person. I'm unique. No one looks or feels exactly the way I do. There isn't a single carbon copy of me in the world.

I believe in a loving God and this makes me feel good. Thanks to my beliefs and the program, I'm not a pawn in a chess game any more. I'm my own person. I'm growing and learning and I have a purpose for living this and every day.

Things to Think About

Before Alateen I always thought I was different. Now I realize that I am—in a very positive way. I'm one of God's miracles. There's no one in the world like me. I'm a worthwhile person, filled with good things, ready to make the most of today.

Before I came to Alateen there were times when I felt very much alone. The more I tried to make sense out of everything that was happening in our home, the more I felt as if I was taking on the world.

Today, thanks to Alateen, I'm an important link in a worldwide chain of love and understanding. These words, from a member in West Germany, remind me just how strong that chain is:

> "It's really something to be part of Alateen where I have real friends who understand me. My new friends and I share a deep feeling for one another."

It's that deep feeling for one another that pulls the Alateen fellowship together all around the world. I'm part of it and I don't have to feel alone anymore.

Things to Think About
Being part of the Alateen fellowship is like having good friends all over the world. Where we live isn't important; we all share the same feelings. That kind of understanding has a way of getting rid of loneliness. It draws us together and makes the miles disappear.

Broken promises and disappointments made me lose faith in people. It's hard to trust someone who has let me down.

Learning to trust again doesn't happen overnight. It takes time because trust is something that has to be earned. It grows when people follow through on their promises to me.

But it has a lot to do with my attitude, too. If I'm willing to give others a second chance and trust them a little more each day, some of that faith in people may start to come back.

Things to Think About

I don't wake up one morning and decide I'm going to trust everybody again. Trust needs time to grow. How other people treat me plays a part in how much I trust them. But the way *I* think can make a difference, too. When I let go of my past disappointments, I can start to have faith in others and give them another chance to reach me today.

I worried about a lot of things, especially while I was in school. Instead of thinking about my schoolwork, I'd worry about my dad; would he be drunk and mean to my family? This didn't help my grades.

Now, I'm learning not to worry about things like that. I'm a lot calmer and it's helped me to concentrate on my work at school, too.

One of the slogans that helps me is "Live and Let Live." I can't do a thing about my dad's behavior, so what's the use of worrying about it? I need to look after my life, schoolwork included, and do the best I can.

Things to Think About

When I worry about things I can't control, I'm only hurting myself. Alateen helps me to stop worrying about other people and their lives so I can make the most of mine. Today I'll concentrate on doing the best I can with me and I won't have time to worry about things that are out of my hands.

I can't accomplish much of anything when I'm frustrated. My thinking is scrambled and my feelings are stirred up. I start reacting to everything and I take my frustrations out on everybody around me.

When I get upset, I need to take a minute to slow down and ask myself if it's really that important. Relaxing helps me get rid of the tension that builds up inside of me and I start to think a lot more clearly.

Being frustrated gives me a chance to look inside myself. I understand how that frustration usually starts because I'm not happy with myself. Alateen shows me how to change that, so I don't have to let my frustration get the better of me or anyone else.

Things to Think About

Being frustrated paralyzes my thinking. The more I struggle, the worse it gets. The program has an answer: relax and put things into perspective. As peace of mind takes over, there's just no room for frustration.

I was a great one for opening my mouth too quickly. I said and did things that I later regretted. I made rush decisions, forgetting that important things need some careful thought.

The problems I caused could have been avoided if I had just stopped to think things through. Now, with the help of Alateen, that's just what I'm learning to do. When I use the slogan "Think," I can plan things out before I act, and as a result things have a way of working out a lot better.

Things to Think About

Sometimes I talk first and think later and it gets me into trouble. Alateen helps me to turn that around. Using the slogan "Think" helps me think *before* I act and keeps me from saying and doing things I'll be sorry for later.

Who am I? I used to be a clown because people laughed at me and called me names. When they put me down, I tried to become what they wanted me to be.

Now I'm different, thanks to the program. I can be a clown and laugh if I want to, and I can be sad and cry if I have to. I'm a real person again with frowns and fears and in Alateen I don't get put down for being that way.

Who am I? I'm me, and that's who I always want to be.

Things to Think About

People in the fellowship give me the freedom to be me. Instead of trying to do and be what others have in mind for me, I can be the person *I* want to be. With the program to guide me, I can be myself and become something better than I ever thought possible.

When a carpenter wants to create something beautiful out of a piece of plain wood, he has to use the right tools. He has to know what's in his tool-box and to be familiar with how each piece works. In order to get the best use of each tool, he has to keep it in good working order. That means taking care of it and using it as often as he can.

We're a lot like that carpenter in his workshop. Conference Approved Literature is one of the tools in the program. If we leave it on the shelf and never bother using it in our meetings or in our personal lives, our recovery program could get rusty and in need of repair. If we get to know what's in our literature, read a little each day, and try to apply the ideas to our lives, it can be another way to grow in the program. We can take a life that seems plain and dull and turn it into something beautiful.

Things to Think About

Conference Approved Literature can be an important tool in my recovery. It's really just another way that members of the fellowship share their experience, strength, and hope with me. I can get the most out of it when I'm willing to read it and *use* it in my life every day.

There are many ways of not dealing with my problems. I can retreat from them and try to ignore them or find a detour around them. But there isn't much point in that. I can't roll myself into a small enough ball or cover my eyes or hold my ears long enough to make the problems go away. And besides, if I keep stepping back to avoid dealing with my troubles, I'll miss the best part of my life—*living.*

So what do I have to do? First, I have to recognize there's a problem. Looking at the problem as though it belonged to somebody else can help me see how I might handle it from there. I can examine the facts, talk about it, and try to find some answers. Then, I can get on with doing something about putting the answers into action and changing what I can—me.

Things to Think About

I can only run away from my problems for so long before they finally catch up with me. Instead of wasting my time and energy trying to escape from them, wouldn't it be easier if I looked at them honestly in the first place? It makes good sense. When I do that, I can look for some solutions that are right for me and start acting on them.

For a long time I didn't understand how I could both love and hate my alcoholic parent. When things were going well and he cared about me, I felt really good about him. But when a crisis came up and he didn't seem concerned about me at all, I hated him. I was confused. I switched my feelings back and forth so many times that it started to make me sick.

The program showed me that I can't let *my* feelings be controlled by the alcoholic's behavior. When I started to understand his illness, it helped me to stop reacting to his moods. Now I realize that it was really the drinking I hated and I love the alcoholic as a person a lot more than I thought.

Things to Think About

Like a coin the alcoholic has two sides: the side that's genuinely interested in me and loves me, and the side that's interested in getting another drink. If I keep "flipping" to match the side the alcoholic is showing, a lot of my mixed feelings will keep coming back. But when I try to understand the disease and accept him as he is, I can love him regardless of which side turns up.

At one time I had a hard time praying. I was afraid of God and thought He wasn't interested in what I had to say. I heard a lot of fancy words, but every time I tried to say them, they just wouldn't come out. Finally, I gave up trying.

When I came to the fellowship, I learned a lot about prayer in Step Eleven. There was something simple about it, something that said, "Be yourself and tell your Higher Power what you're feeling." There was no guarantee that He'd fix everything, but talking to Him felt better than keeping everything bottled up inside.

I find it easier to pray now. Sometimes I pray on my knees, but I can pray while I'm walking to school, sitting at home, or in a class, too. I'm learning that prayer isn't just thought and words; it's my actions as well. In fact, how I live today can be the highest form of prayer in my life.

Things to Think About

Prayer is a simple, natural thing that can happen anywhere. I don't need a lot of special words, just an honest desire to talk to my Higher Power. Putting the "talk" into action can make my prayers come alive!

When an alcoholic first finds sobriety, we think our troubles are over. Then some of us find that a sober alcoholic can be as hard to live with as a drinking one. And we're not sure we like it.

We've spent a long time waiting for the alcoholic to stop drinking. Now that he has, we're still not happy. We think we deserve more. We know he's trying hard to stay sober, but we resent the fact that his moods are so hard to handle. Sometimes we think things were better when he was drinking.

We need the program now more than ever to get our thinking straightened out. Instead of feeling sorry for ourselves, we can be grateful that the alcoholic is sober. We can accept the fact that sobriety isn't the answer to all our problems and use the program to start dealing with the changes it brings.

Things to Think About

Sometimes it seems that sobriety may bring even more problems than I had when the alcoholic was drinking. When I practice the program, I get a clearer picture. It's tough, at times, because of all the changes, but I'd rather have sobriety than drinking any day. Today I'll be grateful for the sobriety in our home and work on my attitude so I can adjust to this new way of life.

I used to talk a lot at school about my problems. Most people listened and felt sorry for me. I'd say things like, "My dad is an alcoholic." It made me feel better until one day, somebody told me to listen and reminded me that I wasn't the only person in the world with problems. It was then that I started to realize I'd been blaming my father for every problem I had.

I came to Alateen a short time later and heard people talking about "playing the martyr." The description fit me perfectly. I'd been bragging about my troubles to gain attention from everyone and I'd actually enjoyed the attention and pity I was getting from them. In Alateen I learned to stop playing games and recognize my self-pity for what it really was.

Things to Think About

Sometimes I feel important when I complain about all the tough times I'm going through. Now I can see right through that—it's nothing more than self-pity. When I stop feeling sorry for myself and get to work on the program, I'll be able to help other people who *are* still—suffering.

Living with an alcoholic made me feel "off-balance" a lot of the time. I was never sure what was going on to happen next and I couldn't even guarantee my own actions.

Sometimes my shortcomings would get the best of me and I'd start reacting to everything. It seemed as though I had two left feet and every time I opened my mouth, I'd say something wrong. I felt like I was one big mistake!

Alateen reminds me that everybody makes mistakes. I know now that it isn't the end of the world when *I* make one. It doesn't have to upset me and ruin everything I'm doing. If I want to, I can learn from my mistakes and use them to help me grow. The greatest growth comes when I try to remember that *I* am not a mistake just because I make one.

Things to Think About

I make a lot of mistakes every day. There's nothing wrong with that unless I let them get me down. With the help of the program, I don't have to do that anymore. Instead, I can share with other Alateen members and let the mistakes open the door to learning more about myself.

Most of my life, before Alateen, I traveled many roads. Each one seemed to lead in a different direction. I was used to doing things my way and if a route looked good to me, I'd take it without mapping it out or checking conditions. I found the roads confusing and rough, long and not very pleasant. Most of the time I'd end up lost or at a dead end.

Through Alateen, and with the help of the people in the program, I've learned to map out my route before I start each day. I check the road conditions and follow directions and I try to be more aware of the obstacles I might meet along the way. It's a lot easier to travel now and my mind is free to enjoy everything that passes my way.

Things to Think About

"Traveling" the Alateen way is the best way for me to go. With the Steps and Traditions as my signposts, I know I'm on the right road, going in the right direction. My destination: Recovery.

Alateen is a lot like playing tennis—one day while I was warming up, I realized the backboard returned to me the kind of shot I hit to it. If I made a good shot, I got a good one back. If my shot was poor, the return was the same. It's that way with my program, too. If I try to work the program in everything I do, it works for me. But if I don't, the results aren't that great.

Later in the week, while I was playing a game, my racket broke. I knew I should get rid of it, but I was determined to keep going and grew more frustrated with every shot I made. It reminded me of the days before Alateen when I tried to do things by using *my* will. It wasn't the best "piece of equipment," but I didn't care. I just kept on going, getting more upset all the time. Then Alateen introduced me to the Twelve Steps, a reliable "piece of equipment," which doesn't fail.

Things to Think About

What I put into the program will determine what I get out of it. If I grit my teeth and try to solve my problems in my own way, I'm looking for trouble. But when I use the Twelve Steps, I'll get the most out of the program each day.

Before Alateen my attitude and behavior changed with the people I was with. I thought I had to agree with everybody and act the same way they did. When I was around rowdy people, I acted loud and mouthy. If I was with someone quiet, I was nice and well-mannered. When I was in the company of church people, I gave up swearing and tried to appear very holy. Around tough people, I thought I should act tough, too. I was trying to be all things to all people. The trouble is—I never really knew who *I* was.

Today I'm my own person thanks to the program. My personality is based on what *I* think and who *I* am. I don't have to change every time I'm with somebody different. I'm a quiet person by nature and that's just fine. I can be that way no matter who I'm with and hope they'll respect me for it. If they don't, that's their problem not mine because I have my self-respect and I'm happy with who I am today.

Things to Think About

If I try to be a carbon copy of other people, I'll never get to know who I really am. When I stick to the original, I'll find out that I'm more exciting to be with than I thought. The program gives me the power to be me—someone unique and terrific. It's up to me to believe it.

I don't remember much about my father's drinking. He's been sober for a long time. My mother has been in Al-Anon for about the same length of time. Both of them told me I had to go to Alateen because it would be good for me. I didn't like the idea, but I went to meetings to keep them happy. After awhile I started to have thoughts like, "Why am I going?" I decided I could get along without the meetings so I quit.

Then my whole life changed. I'd wake up in a bad mood and stay that way for days at a time. My friends started calling me a snob and told me to get lost every time I went near them. In general, I was feeling down.

I realized how much I needed Alateen. I've started going to meetings again because *I* want to go, not because someone else tells me I have to go. I see now that I'm not going to Alateen just because I have an alcoholic parent; I'm going because the program can make a big difference in *my* life.

Things to Think About

Am I in Alateen because I want to be? Other people can tell me to go, but I'm the one who has to make the choice about how much I get out of it. When *I* choose to attend meetings and live the program, I'm the one who benefits because I choose to grow.

I used to spend a lot of time concentrating on the negative parts of my life. I envied people who had more spending money, nicer homes, sober parents, and brothers and sisters who didn't annoy one another. I thought my life was terrible and I let everybody know about it.

Then I came to Alateen and had the chance to see how other kids dealt with their home life. Some who had the most to be thankful for were often grumpy and miserable. I saw a lot of myself in them and didn't like it at all. Others, who really had miserable lives, tried to keep a smile on their faces and get some happiness out of what little they had. They made me realize there was more to life than complaining.

It's true that the problems at home can sometimes get me down. But I don't have to feel sorry for myself because of what's going on. Instead, I can concentrate on being thankful for the good things I do have.

Things to Think About

Alcoholism can be tough on me. If I'm still feeling sorry for myself, I don't have time for my own growth. Maybe it's time I woke up and realized that I *can* shut off the old self-pity routine, change my attitude, and try to be a bit more cheerful each day. Before long I may discover that it really does work!

Sometimes I feel as if I'm running in circles going a hundred miles an hour. I can't seem to think straight. I rush around, letting things pile up until I'm forced to make spur-of-the-moment decisions, which often turn out poorly.

Then I remember "Easy Does It." It works wonders for me because it helps me to slow down. I let go of the things that bother me and think before I act. When I'm more relaxed, I can get on with my day.

Things to Think About

Today I'll try to settle down and think before I act. I'll be good to myself and take things as they come.

Resentment is one of the hardest feelings to let go of. It gets a hold on our thinking that's tough to break. It hurts us and other people, too.

Through the program, I'm learning to take care of my resentments before they get the best of me. Using slogans like "How Important Is It?" and "Let Go and Let God" really helps me to deal with them.

If a resentment is too big for me to handle myself, I call on my Alateen friends. Talking it over helps me to calm down and see things more clearly. These friends don't give me fast answers or tell me what to do. They just listen and share how they've taken care of some of their resentments. And that gives me the push I need to work things out for myself.

Things to Think About

Resentment is a strong feeling. If I let it take control of me today, I'll end up hurting myself and the people around me. Talking about my resentments with my fellow Alateens will help me get a better picture of things. I'll start to relax and let go of my angry feelings.

One of the first things I heard when I came to Alateen was the word "disease." I'd never thought of my mother's drinking as a disease and at first I didn't believe it. I told myself I'd have to learn more about alcoholism before I accepted that idea.

I listened at meetings and I read Alateen and Al-Anon literature. Gradually I started to understand a lot more about alcoholism, how it affected my mother and why it made our family life so miserable. Understanding made it easier for me to take a look at Step One and admit that I was powerless over alcohol.

Now I can accept my mother as a person. I realize that she really does have a disease and that only she can handle it. I'm still trying to learn as much as I can about it, but right now my own recovery is the most important thing for me. I'm working on it by using the tools of the program.

Things to Think About

Before the program I thought the alcoholic was just an unkind, unloving, and cruel person who drank too much. Now I understand she has a disease. Only she can do something about it. I've been affected, too, and thanks to Alateen, *I* can do something about changing *me*.

Sometimes I don't know what to do about a problem. I become frustrated because I can't solve it by myself. I look to the people in the program and as much as they try to help me, it just doesn't seem to work. I know there's a solution, but I can't always find it.

Usually I'm too wrapped up in the problem to see where the answer lies. But when I step back and get a better picture of things, the solution is obvious: the first four Steps. In the first three, I let go of the problem by saying, "I can't, He can, and I think I'll let Him." I start to realize I'm the cause of most of my problems so I take my inventory to change the way I think and act. With time and a little bit of patience, the problem usually takes care of itself.

Things to Think About

When I'm trying to solve a problem, Steps One, Two, and Three help me to put the problem into the best hands. Then I use Step Four to start working on it. For *every* problem I have today, there's an answer in the Steps.

After working on the first four Steps, I thought the Fifth Step was going to be easy. Telling God and another person that things weren't right inside of me couldn't be all that bad. I could even admit some things to myself.

But admitting the *exact nature of my wrongs* wasn't easy at all. I had to dig deep to find out *why* I was the way I was. Take anger for instance, It was easy for me to say that I get angry because other people make me feel that way. But the truth is that I only get angry because I allow myself to. It has nothing to do with other people and everything to do with me.

Step Five helped me accept the truth about myself. When I faced up to the real me, it was a lot easier to get at the root of my problems and that gave me the start I needed to get rid of them.

Things to Think About

Honesty makes Step Five work the way it does. I stop pretending and I admit the truth to God, to myself, and to another person. I get rid of the things I'd like to believe about myself and the things I want others to believe about me, and I focus on what's really true. When I look deep inside of myself and ask why, I find the real answers I need to work out my defects of character.

When I was a newcomer to Alateen, I used to ask, "Why does an alcoholic drink?" I was always afraid that I had caused the drinking problem in our home and wanted to know what I could do to stop it.

I was told there are probably as many answers to that question as there are alcoholics in the world. But the simple truth is an alcoholic drinks because he is an alcoholic. It has nothing to do with me. What a relief!

Now I realize it's not important to know *why* an alcoholic drinks—just to accept the fact that he does and that drinking causes problems. I know I'm not to blame for the problem and there's nothing I can do to stop the drinking since it wasn't me who started it in the first place.

Things to Think About

Why an alcoholic drinks is anybody's guess. Thanks to the program, I know I'm *not* one of the reasons. When I start to accept alcoholism as an illness, I'll stop trying to answer questions about alcoholism and get on with asking some important ones about myself.

Before I found Alateen I was lonely and scared. I felt embarrassed and ashamed and was convinced that my family was different—no one else had a drinking problem in their family.

In the meetings I've met a lot of other teenagers with the same feelings I had. Our problems are pretty much the same so I don't have to be embarrassed and ashamed any more. I feel free to talk about what's on my mind, and the understanding and help I get is just what I need to straighten out my life, if I'm willing to use it.

Things to Think About

Knowing that other people are going through the same things I am makes my life a lot easier today. We all help each other by sharing our feelings and by listening and caring. That's what makes Alateen such a great program!

A message from one Alateen group:

"We found out the hard way that having more than one purpose only weakens the message of Alateen. Our group decided it would be a good idea to give our members a chance to socialize so we started having dances after the meetings. Pretty soon the word got around and the kids were coming just for the dance and not for the meeting. The plans for the dance got to be so important that the meeting was forgotten or the members were only halfhearted about it.

"Eventually the group got together and decided to get rid of the dances. You can go dancing lots of other places, but you can only get the Alateen program at an Alateen meeting."

Things to Think About

We get together to help each other and to reach out to teenagers who need to hear about Alateen. If we want the real message of the program to get through, we need to take Alateen seriously in our own lives *and* in our group. Tradition Five holds the key to making it happen.

I went to my first meeting looking for answers to my mother's problems. She wouldn't do anything to solve them so I took it upon myself to find the answers.

I soon found out that Alateen didn't have those kinds of answers. At first I felt like turning around and walking out the way I'd come in. But because Alateen was the last place I could go, I decided to stick around and give the program a try.

I'm glad I did. I realize now that the program has a lot of answers—*for me*. When I put them into action in my life, I learn to take care of myself and let my mother find her answers in her own way and time.

Things to Think About

I'm searching for answers all the time. I'll find lots of them if I'm willing to use the program. The answers are for me, no one else. I may have to dig a little bit to find them, but the digging I do is the thing that makes me a strong and growing person today.

Many times we feel hurt because our parents seem to treat us as though they don't really love us. Often what they're saying isn't what we're hearing. Sometimes we're just too stubborn to listen or talk to them.

If we won't talk to our parents, we're hurting ourselves more than anyone else. If we keep our feelings inside, how can anyone help us? How can people know how we feel if we won't tell them?

No one, not even our parents, can read our minds. It's up to us to tell them how we feel *and* to spend some time listening to them, too.

Things to Think About

I learn a lot through communicating with other people. Sharing feelings with them—talking and listening—helps to get rid of the "static" on our lines of communication. Alateen helps to *keep* those lines clear.

I used to expect a lot from other people. When they couldn't deliver, I'd put them down. I thought it was pretty harmless until they turned on me. That's when I started to develop some big resentments.

When I came to Alateen, I heard a lot of talk about accepting other people. At first I didn't want to accept anybody because of the way I'd been treated. After awhile I started thinking I could put up with other people if I had to. At the time, that was my idea of acceptance. Now I know it was a long way from it.

I had to change my attitude. In the beginning, I practiced on the people in my group. As I learned to accept these new friends, it helped me to accept the people I still resented. I tried to stop expecting too much from them and eventually some of us even started getting along again.

Things to Think About

Acceptance is more than just tolerating other people. It's the kind of attitude that makes me feel good inside. It lets me give people the freedom to be what they really are instead of expecting them to be what *I* think they should be. When I stop trying to get from people what they can't give me, I can accept them and enjoy all they have to offer.

Some people think Alateen is for young alcoholics. Others say it's a gossip and gripe session where kids talk about their parents. Still others think Alateen is just a social gathering for teens while some feel it's a baby-sitting service for parents when they go to a meeting.

None of this is true. But even if a few people think this way, a lot of potential Alateen members may not get the help they need.

That's why it's up to each of us to do our part to make sure people get the right picture of our fellowship. We've been affected by alcoholism and we need help. By using the tools of the program, we're able to sort out our own lives. Showing that in our action is the strongest message we can carry.

Things to Think About

A few bad examples can give people the wrong impression about what Alateen really is. It's surprising how hard it is to change their minds. Alateen means a lot to me and I want to do what I can to attract people to it. If I take the program seriously and show what it's done for me, the message of the program will come through loud and clear and people just might like what they see and hear.

Blaming people, places, and things is almost a way of life for many of us who are children of alcoholics. We blame schools for having rules, teachers for expecting us to learn, and churches for not helping us. We blame our parents for not loving us enough, for giving us too much or too little, and most of all we blame ourselves for causing the drinking.

We seem to think that if only *they* would change, everything in our lives would straighten out. But is that true? Do we need to wait for people, places and things to change?

Alateen's answer is loud and clear: "Let It Begin With Me." We learn to accept responsibility for our own lives instead of blaming others. If we wait around for other people to change, they may never do it and we'll miss a lifetime of chances to grow. It's up to us to make the most of our lives today.

Things to Think About

It's easy to blame other people for what's wrong in my life. It takes the pressure off me. But Alateen helps me put things in the right perspective: I'm in charge of my own life. If I want things to go right today, *I* have to take the action to make it happen.

I lived for the day when I could move out and get away from the problem in our home. I thought I could put that part of my life behind me and get on with real living the way my friends were doing. When I finally did move out, I got the surprise of my life. I hadn't left my problems behind me at all; I'd taken them with me. I worried all the time, especially about my younger sisters and brothers and about whether my mother would be able to cope with the situation at home without my help. I couldn't concentrate on my own life and bit-by-bit I started to fall apart.

I came to the fellowship just in time. I had to admit that moving away hadn't solved a thing because I couldn't run away from myself. Now I'm trying to meet my problems head on and deal with them one at a time. I've told my family about the program, too, and let them know I love them and I'm here if they need me. I'm also learning to detach and let them face their own problems.

Things to Think About

Escaping from my problems by leaving home just isn't worth it. Most times I end up feeling worse than ever because I worry. For a change, I'll try to "hang in there" and work out my problems. That takes a lot more courage and I'll have a lot more respect for myself if I do.

Before I came to Alateen I always tried so hard to impress everybody. I did everything I could to make people like me and when they didn't, I thought I was awful. Everything bad that happened to me, even the smallest things, seemed like the end of the world.

Today I have the benefit of Alateen. Before I get my mind twisted about everything, I ask myself, "How Important Is It?" I don't have to get all wound up and ruin the whole day. Instead I can relax, let people like me as I am, and take things as they come.

Things to Think About

Making a big deal about little things is a waste of my time and energy. Today I'll use the slogan "How Important Is It?" It will help me think things through before I act and it will give me a better picture of just what *is* important in my life.

I have a right to feel happy. Nobody can take that away from me. I have as good a chance as anybody else for a happy life. It all depends on my attitude.

There's an alcoholic in my family. That makes it harder to be happy, but not impossible. That fact can't take away my right to be happy unless I let it.

Happiness isn't a matter of chance. It has nothing to do with where I live or the people around me. It's an inside job. I make my own happiness based on how I feel about my life.

Things to Think About

It's a waste of time waiting for other people to make me feel good. My happiness depends on how *I* think. Today, I'll take time to think about the things that make me happy and realize that my happiness is in my own hands.

At one time I blamed myself for everything that went wrong in my life. I felt terrible. But after awhile I convinced myself that it was all God's fault. That made me feel better because it was now His fault, and I was no longer to blame for how things turned out.

When I came to Step Three there was no way I was going to turn my will and my life over to God. He'd done a lousy job up to that time, I thought, so why should I expect any improvement? Nobody but me was going to control my life.

Things are different now. It took me awhile, but I finally started to understand what the problem was. I'd been so busy blaming God for mistakes that I couldn't hear what He was really saying. I guess I wasn't a very good listener. I'm still not the best listener, but by coming into closer contact with God, things are much better.

Things to Think About

Blaming God is an easy way out of my problems, but it doesn't do a thing for my relationship with Him. Step Three shows me how to work together with God and let Him help me look after my life.

I had a lot of fears about the alcoholic when I first came to Alateen. These fears clouded my mind so much, it felt as if I had a hangover. Over and over I asked myself, "What if she drinks tonight and gets into a car accident?" What if she loses her job? Is she ever going to join A.A. and get sober?"

The program helped me realize it was a waste of my time to ask such questions as these. It made me take a good look at myself instead. When I did, I began finding out why I was so afraid. I then turned to a Power greater than myself and asked for help to get rid of my fears.

Today, fear doesn't control my thinking. I know there's nothing I can do about the alcoholic's drinking. I'm powerless over it. She may be one of the unfortunate ones who will never stop drinking. I can accept that, too, and try to have compassion for her instead of allowing myself to have another "fear hangover."

Things to Think About

My fears about alcoholism can keep me thinking in circles. The program helps me break their hold on my mind. I find out what my fears are and ask my Higher Power to help me overcome them. Letting go of fear gives me the freedom to work on gaining a better understanding of myself and the alcoholic.

In Alateen we find out what real friendship is all about. By being honest and open and sharing our problems at meetings, we get close to each other.

This kind of friendship opens a lot of new doors. Our confidence grows. We get involved in new activities and meet new people. We get along better with our family and we start to do better in school. In a special way, we begin to feel that life is worth living after all.

Things to Think About

A wise person once said, "Friends are gifts we give oursleves." It could have been said about Alateen. The friendships I've made in my group have shown me that people really do care. They've helped me to have good feelings about myself and that gives me the confidence to move forward.

Living with an alcoholic nearly pushed me "over the edge." I was sure God had abandoned me so I gave up on Him and tried to think things out for myself. By doing this, everything seemed to go from bad to worse. I felt as if I were alone, carrying a heavy load up a steep hill.

In desperation I came to Alateen. It took a long time before I could feel anything at all. Eventually I found a faith in a Power greater than myself. It's different than anything I've ever experienced. It's like a partnership—He supplies the wisdom and I do the leg work—and today it seems to be working out really well.

Things to Think About

At one time my life was one struggle after another because I had no faith. Today I need the program to make my faith work. I can't imagine life without it now. It's that good feeling of knowing there's a real Power behind me, helping me grow every day.

My parents were in A.A. when I came to Alateen. I didn't have a lot of the trouble some Alateens were having living with an active alcoholic. I thought living the program was easy with sobriety at home. Because I was coasting, I wasn't really *living* the program for me at all.

Then someone reminded me that what I get out of the program depends on me, not whether the alcoholic is drinking or sober. That's when I finally woke up and realized I had a lot of growing to do. I started to apply the program to myself. I uncovered feelings I didn't even know were there—fear, resentment, anger, frustration—and tried to deal with them by using the Steps and slogans.

Now I think of sobriety as a kind of added bonus. It isn't a guarantee to smooth sailing; it's just another beginning. I have to work the program just the same as everyone else if I expect it to work for me.

Things to Think About

It's easy to hide behind my parents' sobriety and forget about working the program. But I'll only be denying myself a chance to grow if I do. Instead I'll be grateful for sobriety and think of it as a good place to start. I'll "come out of hiding" today and start living the program for me.

Until I came to Alateen I didn't think anyone had a problem as bad as mine. That gave me plenty of reason to feel sorry for myself.

As I attended more meetings, my eyes started to open. Other people's problems made mine look small, but they were facing theirs with courage. Some kids were in situations as bad as mine, but they didn't act as though it was the end of the world; they accepted the fact that the alcoholic in their lives was suffering from a disease and started doing something about themselves.

Opening my eyes to the problems of other people has stopped my flood of self-pity. I use the program now to work on my problems. I know there's no easy solution to them, but facing them and working them out is a lot better than sitting back and feeling sorry for myself.

Things to Think About

Self-pity is no solution to my problems. Other people have troubles, too, but they don't sit around feeling sorry for themselves. They use the program to do something about their problems. It's time I did something about mine.

Some people can be so phony. I should know: I used to be that way. I was always pretending things were better than they were. I wore a fake smile and lied through my teeth about how I felt inside.

In Alateen I've learned to be real. That means being honest with myself and everybody else. When I'm feeling down, I can show other people that I'm hurting and accept their help. And when I'm happy, I can share that, too, and tell them how good it feels.

I don't have to be a pretender anymore. There's nothing to fake. Thanks to the program, things really *are* better.

Things to Think About

After years of covering up the truth, it's good to know I can show the world the real me. Some days I feel happy, some days I feel sad. But knowing that I'm accepted just the way I am is the best feeling of all.

Learning to live just for today isn't easy. Some of us spend a lot of time worrying about the past and the future.

We rush around so much that we don't let ourselves relax enough to enjoy each day. We jam homework, tests, part-time jobs, dating, and friends into those twenty-four hours and then we realize that sometimes it just can't be done. We become frustrated and worn out.

"One Day at a Time" is a simple slogan for complicated people like us! It helps us to "slow down and live." We start to think straight again and get our lives back in shape. We learn to set priorities, slow down, and enjoy each day as it comes.

Things to Think About

Yesterday is gone and tomorrow isn't here. Today is the only day I have to live. It's like a twenty-four hour time capsule. If I take one in the morning, with a "glass" of positive attitude, I'll relax and get the most out of the day.

I was the kind of person who needed to have things proved to me before I'd believe them. It was like that with my belief in God. I wouldn't accept what other people were saying because they couldn't show me God.

I did a lot of searching on my own. I read books, talked to religious people, meditated, and spent time thinking, but I couldn't find the answers I was looking for.

I had a hard time, even after I came to the fellowship. The Twelve Steps gave me some direction, but I still wasn't satisfied. Then it came to me one night while I was sitting at a meeting. As I watched my fellow members reach out to comfort a troubled newcomer, I knew I'd found what I was looking for; God works through people.

Things to Think About

I don't need books and fancy theories to prove that my Higher Power exists. If I take time to look around at my Alateen meeting, I'll see all the evidence I need. Members reaching out to each other, loving and helping one another; I *know* now that my Higher Power is very real.

How well am I practicing my program? Do I take what I like from my meetings and put it to use or do I just store it away until the next meeting? Do my books and pamphlets lay around the house or do I take time to read them and learn about the program? Do I only share with people at meetings or do I keep in touch with other members and talk things over between meetings?

Questions like these might be part of my Tenth Step each night. Answering them honestly will remind me that working the program takes *daily* practice. It means applying the principles of the program in all my affairs, not just when I'm at a meeting.

Things to Think About

It's easy to be a good member at meetings. But using the program each day is a different story. Taking a daily inventory, with the help of Step Ten, starts me thinking about how much I practice the program.

I came to Alateen looking for love and acceptance from others because I'd given up on myself. I found it when the group welcomed me and made me feel as though I belonged. It was a good feeling, but it wasn't enough to keep me coming back; I needed more.

That's when I started using the Twelve Steps. They took me beyond that "good feeling" and gave me a path to follow so I could start my recovery.

At first the Steps helped me cope with living with an alcoholic. Today I work them at a deeper level. Each experience that I have helps me to understand how these Steps can be applied to *all* parts of my life.

I used to think I had to understand each Step perfectly before I moved on to the next one. Now I just keep moving on through the Steps, trying to use them in everything I do so I can keep growing and recovering each day.

Things to Think About

The good feelings I get from belonging to Alateen are like "icing on the cake." The Twelve Steps are the real meat of the program. They're easy to say and hard to do, but they give me the direction I need to make something of my life. Today I'll start to practice them and be more serious about my recovery.

Step One seems like admitting defeat. I thought I could make the alcoholic stop drinking, but I can't. It's like fighting a losing battle.

I've been trying to control his life for so long that my own is getting out of hand. I'm not looking after myself the way I should, I'm not doing very well in school, and I don't have many friends. I feel as if I can't do anything right. Every time I try to manage things on my own, I really mess them up.

I don't like to think of myself as a loser, but I have to face up to it if I'm ever going to be a "winner" again. Accepting all this is hard to do; Step One can help.

Things to Think About

Trying to control someone else's drinking is like batting zero. Step One is a new beginning. When I'm not afraid to admit that I'm a loser, it can be a start toward working on a "winning streak" for the future.

Step One showed me that my life is like a team that's losing every game. It needs a new manager. Step Two helps me to find that new Manager, a Power greater than myself that can give me a new sense of direction.

I tried to manage my own life, but it was too much for me to handle alone. I needed help.

My new Manager can give me the help I need. He helps to straighten out my thinking and get "the team" working together again. But it's up to me to have enough faith to let Him help me.

Things to Think About

A good team needs a good manager to bring out the best in it. It's the same with my life. I've tried to manage things on my own; that didn't work out. Now, with the help of Step Two, I've found a new Manager—a Higher Power who can take care of my life. With His help, we'll be a "winning team" soon.

I'm so used to managing my own life that it's hard letting someone else take over. But I know that if I keep trying to control things by myself, I'm going to keep on losing.

Step Two asked me to trust my Higher Power to do a good job with my life. That much I can do. But letting go and letting Him *do* the job is another thing. Step Three asks me to make a decision about it. It's hard not to get frightened about it. Letting go is a big risk. If I remember that a good team has *one* good leader, it's a little easier.

I can't really let go completely yet. That's okay. All I'm asked to do is *decide* to do that. If I can do that much, the rest of the Steps will show me how to put the decision into action.

Things to Think About

I still want to control my own life. That makes it hard to let go. Today, with the help of Step Three, I'll decide to do that and let my Higher Power show me what I need. Making the decision will be the beginning of letting *Him* take care of me.

A new manager of a team usually wants to take stock to see what kind of team he's got. It's the same with my Higher Power. When I let go and start to let Him take over, He gets things moving. He wants me to use Step Four to take a good look at myself.

I've needed a good housecleaning for a long time. Once in a while, when I was managing things, I *thought* about cleaning up my act; but it was never enough. Now I have to go deeper than that.

It's kind of scary. It helps to remember that not everything inside of me is bad. I do have some good qualities.

I can't do it all at once. The important thing is doing it. I don't have to do it alone because my Higher Power is there to help me do my best. I know that even though it's hard to face at times, whatever I find can only help to improve me.

Things to Think About

If I was serious about turning my will and my life over to my Higher Power in Step Three, the Fourth Step will get me moving in that direction. It helps me face the real facts about what kind of shape I'm in and get ready to work with my Higher Power to make things better.

In Step Four I found out some of my faults were keeping my good qualities from showing. Now, in Step Five, I need to ask "Why?" and talk about exactly what's going wrong.

First I have to talk with my Higher Power; He's a great listener. He wants me to be honest with Him *and* with myself. It takes time to get over that guilty feeling because of all the things I've done. But when I face the real me, it's easier to accept myself as I am.

He also brings in other people to talk to, usually someone I can trust. When I sit down with that person, it gives me another perspective on things. Sometimes I'm harder on myself than I need to be. Having another listener helps me to see things more clearly.

Things to Think About

Once I've seen my mistakes in Step Four, the only way to get to work on them is to face up to them. Step Five is my chance to do that. Talking things over with my Higher Power and another person and admitting my faults to myself, helps me to understand *why* I feel and act the way I do.

Getting rid of my defects is tough. They don't want to let go and I'm not sure I want them to go. Sometimes they're a good excuse for my poor performance.

I tried to eliminate them on my own, but I couldn't. That's the job of my Higher Power, but He won't do a thing until I'm willing.

Step Six shows me that getting ready is just as important as removing my faults. I wouldn't go out on an important date or play in a big game without preparing myself; it's the same with getting rid of my defects. Once I *am* ready and stop using them as a crutch, my Higher Power can help me.

Things to Think About

If I want to get rid of my defects, I have to stop making excuses and be willing to apply Step Six. When I'm ready, my Higher Power will give me the help I need.

Now that I'm ready to get rid of my faults, Step Seven shows me how to go about it. My Higher Power is ready to help, but it's up to me to ask Him.

Asking Him is a humbling experience. I used to be ashamed to ask anyone for help; it made me feel small and weak. But now I know the truth—*I need help*—I can't do it alone and I'm not afraid to admit it.

My Higher Power has what it takes to get rid of my defects. I'd like Him to take them all away right now. But I have to remember that it took a long time for me to get where I am now; I can't expect to change overnight.

I have to do my part, too. If I sit around and take it for granted that He will always help me, my old problems will be back in no time. But if I try to replace each of my shortcomings with a new quality I'd like to have, I'll be free to enjoy the good things in me each day.

Things to Think About

I need the help of my Higher Power to remove my faults. He's ready to help me, but I have to *ask* Him. Getting rid of my shortcomings is more than just having them taken away; it's replacing them with the good things He would like me to be. Today, with His help, a better me is within reach.

In the past, I hurt a lot of people: family, friends, and even innocent spectators. Step Eight gets me ready to make amends to them. It's like Step Six because it shows me that *getting ready* is just as important as *doing it.*

Part of getting ready is putting the names on a list. It's easy for me to say that everything was "their" fault. But writing names down helps me to face up to the fact that I hurt other people.

Making my list won't mean a thing unless I'm willing to do something with it. I can put it off, and make a lot of excuses, but my Higher Power won't let me do that. He wants me to be *willing* to apologize so that when the time comes to make my amends, I'll be a lot more honest and sincere.

Things to Think About

I've hurt a lot of people and I feel badly about it. I know I need to apologize to them, but I have to be willing to do it before I can really mean it. Step Eight gets me there. When I've put together a list and I've really thought seriously about making my amends, I'll be ready to say an honest, "I'm sorry!"

By the time I finished making my list in Step Eight, I realized I'd forgotten one important person—*me*. I hurt myself a lot by all the problems I caused.

Step Nine helps me to forgive myself. I don't always feel I deserve to be forgiven, but when I remember that my Higher Power forgives me, it's easier to forgive myself and ask other people for their forgiveness.

A simple "I'm sorry" can be a start. Even if it's rejected, I know I've done my best to put the past to rest.

Sometimes other people can be hurt by bringing up the past. That's when I have to let go and let God.

Things to Think About

I learn a lot about forgiveness from the Ninth Step. Forgiving myself makes it easier to ask other people to forgive me. Most of them will when I go directly to them with an honest apology. Making amends to myself and others is a big victory over the past that gives me a chance to start winning again today.

Now that I'm back on the winning track, I want to keep it that way. I can't let things go or I'll be back where I started in no time.

My Higher Power likes a clean slate every day and Step Ten is a good way to start. I have to check out my attitudes and actions regularly to see where things can be improved. When I make a mistake (and I still make plenty of them) I need to admit that I'm wrong right away instead of letting the problems pile up as they did before.

When I keep an eye on things each day, I feel up-to-date. It helps me concentrate on today, instead of trying to make up for the mistakes I made in the past.

Things to Think About

An inventory isn't a one-time deal; it's something I need to do each day to keep myself honest. When I take a look at myself each day and try to take care of problems as they come up, little things don't build up into big problems. That keeps my mind on today and lets me put all my energy into living it.

My Higher Power and I have been through a lot together as we've tried to rebuild my life. But sometimes I don't feel that close to Him. I'd like to get to know Him better. I can, by using Step Eleven.

When I go looking for God, He's not hard to find. He doesn't have an office or sit behind a desk; He's with me all the time. I can talk to Him and He's always ready to listen, even when all I do is complain. Sometimes He wants *me* to listen to Him. That's when I start to understand why He calls the kinds of plays He does.

Sometimes, when I get busy and forget to check in with Him, I start to feel panicky again. He just smiles and gives me a gentle nudge to remind me who's boss. Then He gives me the game plan for the day and lots of strength and confidence to help me carry it out.

Things to Think About

I feel closer to my Higher Power than ever before thanks to the Eleventh Step. He's a great listener and He's always willing to share His plans with me when I'm ready to listen to Him. Sometimes I'm afraid to do things His way. When I remember that He believes in me and is there to help me, I can give it a try.

I have a lot more spirit now because of the Twelve Steps. With the help of my Higher Power, things are really moving ahead. I'm more interested in what I'm doing and I have more energy to do it.

I feel like a winner today! At one time I would have wanted that feeling all for myself. But now, when I look around and see so many people who think they're losers because they live with an alcoholic, I want them to know how to get it. When I reach out, I can help them pull themselves together and make myself a stronger person at the same time.

Things don't end here at Step Twelve. It's really just a beginning because working the program is a daily thing. It's like any good team; to stay in shape I have to keep practicing every day.

Things to Think About

I know that working the Twelve Steps doesn't guarantee I'll win every time. The schedule ahead is bound to have some rough spots, but now I have the courage to *believe* that I'm a winner. Being a winner is more than just a feeling; because of the program, it's an attitude that's part of everything I do in my life today.

"Easy Does It" helps me control myself in tense situations. If I'm taking a test at school and I start rushing through it, thinking about this slogan makes me realize how fast I'm going and helps me slow down.

Saying "Easy Does It" can also be a big help when somebody insults me or calls me names. It reminds me that yelling at the person is only going to get me in trouble.

Even when I get hit or yelled at at home, this slogan can help. When I feel like fighting back and think I'd like to hurt somebody, I take a deep breath, repeat the slogan, and walk away.

Things to Think About

Things happen every day that can make me feel uptight. But when I use "Easy Does It" they don't have to get to me. I can shift into low gear and have a better chance of enjoying the day.

When our group has a problem and one person tries to take over and push an idea on everybody, it hurts the group. No one else has a chance to share ideas and sometimes we end up making decisions without looking at the problem closely enough.

God has the answers for us and He'll guide us in the right direction if we use the group conscience to solve our problems. We have leaders, but they're only trusted servants who carry out what the group wants. *Every* member is important and has the right to speak up. When we work together, we're a *real* group and we all have a share in looking for the answers that will make us strong.

Things to Think About

Group problems need group answers. One person can't decide what's best for the group; we all need to get involved. When we all help to solve problems, *everybody* has a chance to grow. That's the group conscience at work—the way God wants it to be.

I'll never forget the feeling I had at my first meeting. I knew I was in the right place. People understood me and offered to help me. I realized I had a lot of work to do. I was willing to do anything to get what these people had.

I tried hard to change myself, but things weren't moving fast enough for me. Then someone suggested I stop concentrating on changing myself and think first about accepting myself. That gave me the boost I needed.

Now instead of thinking about what I'm "supposed to be," I can enjoy the good feeling of liking me. I still want to change myself, but now I realize that will happen a lot more naturally when I concentrate on accepting myself today.

Things to Think About

I'm not very happy with the way I am right now. I want to make some changes in my life. Before I start doing that, I have to be willing to accept myself as I am. That's the key to finding the courage to change myself into the kind of person I really want to be.

There used to be a communication problem between our Alateen group and Al-Anon and A.A.. We were too busy doing our thing to be interested in what they were doing and we assumed they thought we were just a bunch of kids who were out to cause trouble.

When we took a look at the last part of Tradition Six, things started to change. We invited some Al-Anon and A.A. speakers to one of our open meetings and set up a question-and-answer session so we could talk with each other. We learned how similar we really are. We're all here trying to recover from alcoholism, in one way or another, by following the Twelve Steps.

Now we realize we all need to listen to each other. Hearing A.A. members helps us to understand the alcoholic. Listening to Al-Anon speakers gives us an idea of the nonalcoholic's feelings. And, we can share with them what it feels like to be children of alcoholics. Keeping the lines of communication open helps us understand each other.

Things to Think About

I can learn a lot from Al-Anon and A.A. members. They can help me understand my parents and share with me their ideas about working the program. They can learn from me, too. It all starts with cooperation, the kind that comes from trying to practice Tradition Six. It's the beginning of communication.

When I look back I regret all the time I wasted trying to do things alone. Living with an alcoholic made me feel very lonely. I thought I was on my own; I was sure no one knew how I was feeling.

The program showed me how wrong I was. As I shared with the people in my group, I started to understand that I wasn't alone after all. We're in this together: We have similar feelings and we're all trying to do something with our lives.

After a while I started to apply the slogan "Together We Can Make It." Now I know that I've got my Alateen friends and a God of my understanding on my side. Together we're going to make it!

Things to Think About

Alateen is a together program. It gets us out of ourselves and into sharing with other people. That's how we grow. Today, instead of trying to tackle my problems by myself, I'll let Alateen show me how to work them out together with the help of other people.

My father and I hurt each other a lot. It seemed that no matter how much I changed with the help of the program, there was always a wall between us. I wanted to tell him how I really felt, but I was scared to talk to him because we usually ended up in an argument.

I decided to write my father a letter to tell him my feelings. I told him how his drinking scared me, made me feel angry and resentful, and how it hurt me. I apologized for hurting him and told him I loved him in spite of everything that had happened between us. When I finished the letter, I gave it to him. That took a lot of courage because I'd never been so honest with him before.

I'm glad I wrote it. We're still not that close—we'll probably never be as close as I'd like us to be—but the wall has been broken down a bit and I'm not afraid to be myself with him. For that, I'm glad I took the risk.

Things to Think About

Hurt feelings can put barriers between me and other people. It's not always easy to break those barriers down. But if I have the courage to try, it could open up lines of communication that might have stayed closed forever. Regardless of the outcome, I can be happy knowing I did my best.

Why do I spend so much time trying to make the alcoholic stop drinking? Because he has a disease, he has a craving for alcohol. I can no more stop this by words and actions than I could stop cancer or diabetes.

There is a way I can help: by changing my attitude. I can try to understand the disease and accept the alcoholic as a human being. I can use kind words and thoughtful actions and remember that he already feels guilty enough.

Alateen shows me how to do this by giving me the First Step and the rest of the program to live by. When I stop trying to "cure" the alcoholic and accept him for who and what he is, I can help him the most by simply helping myself.

Things to Think About

Of course I want to help the alcoholic—it's only natural when I see what he's doing to himself. But *how* I help makes a difference. The program shows me I can't control or cure him, but I *can* change my attitude toward him. If I accept alcoholism as an illness today and treat the alcoholic with respect and understanding, I'll be helping myself a lot and that's the best help I can give to the alcoholic.

I have a lot of problems. It's depressing when I think I have to work on them forever, but I *can* do something about them "Just For Today" with the help of the program.

I'll start by thinking of all the good things I have instead of complaining about all the things that seem wrong to me. I can be happy if I want to; the program gives me that choice.

I'll get to work on the Steps and start applying the things I'm learning in the program. People are trying to help me. It's time I let them. Maybe if I learn to be a better listener, I'll hear what they're saying and I might even be able to help other people take care of their problems.

Things to Think About

Sometimes it seems my problems will never be solved. I have to keep working on them, but what I can't do for my whole life, I can do "Just For Today." Applying the program to my life makes my problems a lot more manageable.

The Sponsors of the Alateen group I attend have made it easier for me to think about going from Alateen to Al-Anon. Just by being the kind of members they are, they've shown me how much Al-Anon can do for me.

Sometimes though, fear makes me forget this. I'm afraid I won't fit in. I'm a teenager and they're adults. How can we possibly relate to each other?

My Alateen Group Sponsors understand how I feel. They've told me Al-Anon members have fears, too. But the key is in giving each other a chance. A great place to start is to forget about the age difference and remember that we all have the same kinds of feelings. Sharing those feelings with one another can be the beginning to helping each other grow.

Things to Think About

When I talk about my feelings at an Al-Anon meeting, I know the other members understand. That's the great bond between them and me. It helps me put aside my excuses about being different so I can concentrate on sharing a program of growth.

When my father was sent to prison, I thought I'd be free from all the trouble his drinking had caused me. But I had feelings inside me that kept me locked up in my own kind of prison. I was ashamed when I heard other people talking about their fathers. I hated mine for making me the "man of the house." And deep down, I was scared to death I'd turn out just like he did.

One day, while my mother was visiting at the prison, my father told her that he'd joined A.A. and wanted her to go to Al-Anon and me to go to Alateen. "Why should I?" was my first thought. "He's never done anything for me." But my mother convinced me to give it a try and I'm glad she did.

I've learned that alcoholism isn't something to be ashamed of; it's a disease. I'm not proud my dad is behind bars, but I don't have to spend all my time thinking about it, either. Instead I can start dealing with my feelings about him. The program may not get my dad out of his prison, but it can help *me* stay out of mine.

Things to Think About

I used to live in my own little prison, locked in by my feelings of hatred and shame. Now I'm free. The key is using the program to do something for me.

I used to get a burning feeling inside of me whenever I had a problem with my family or my friends. It was scary. I couldn't look anybody in the eye because I was afraid they'd see it.

In Alateen I found out that this frightening feeling is anger. Anything can set it off and most times there's not much logic to it. But I also learned that it's okay to get angry—to let my feelings out—as long as it doesn't hurt anybody else.

Now I'm finding out I can put my anger to good use. Whenever I get mad, I go running, riding my bike, or simply punch my pillow. These things help me to release my anger instead of letting it build up inside me or taking it out on the people around me. When I'm calmer, I can look at the reasons why I was angry and try to change what I can.

Things to Think About

In Alateen I'm learning that my feelings are important. I have to pay attention to them and not ignore them or squash them down inside of me. Today, when I feel angry, I'll try to let the feelings out and do something constructive with the energy that has built up inside of me.

When I resent other people, why can't I tell them how I feel? What makes it so difficult to let them know what's bothering me?

Fear stops me most of the time. I'm afraid I might say something to hurt their feelings and they'll end up not liking me. I know how much resentment hurts me, but it's hard to do something about it.

Step Four can help. When I take an inventory of myself, I see the cause of my resentment. I take it apart, piece-by-piece, and examine its causes to see what's beneath it. That helps me let go of my negative feelings and gives me the confidence to talk things out.

Things to Think About

When I hide my resentment, I'm the one who gets hurt. I need to get rid of it before it does even more damage. The Fourth Step is a good place to start. It will help me to see what's causing my resentment and get me started on working it out.

Everyone in our home used to take responsibility for other people's feelings. When one of us became upset, we all did. This often resulted in bitter fights.

I thought a lot of the fights were my fault. Sometimes I was afraid to express any feelings at all in case it would set off another argument and hurt someone in my family.

In Alateen I'm learning to express my real feelings. They have less power to affect other people than I thought. Knowing this, I don't have to worry about other people's feelings affecting me either. I realize now that I'm not responsible for the way others feel and they're not responsible for how I feel. That's something I decide for myself.

Things to Think About

Other people have the right to express their feelings, but they can't change *my* feelings unless I want them to. I can't change theirs, either. When I accept this, I'll be free to show my real feelings today and make sure that the way *I* feel is in my own hands, just where I want it to be.

Why do I have to be so careful when it comes to anonymity? To protect myself from being embarrassed? No! A more important reason is that names don't really count. Many times if names are mentioned, the personality comes before the principle. If a good deed is done and a name is attached to that deed, there's a good chance the name will get more recognition than the deed.

Maintaining my anonymity helps me to be humble. I don't need to be recognized by others. My Higher Power recognizes me every day.

Things to Think About

Anonymity helps keep me humble. I don't have to go looking for praise for everything I do. My good feeling comes from knowing that I'm doing what my Higher Power wants me to do.

Many of us tried to be referees. We were torn between the alcoholic and the nonalcoholic, thinking we had to take sides. We took part in arguments, fighting for one side and then the other, and ended up confused and frustrated.

For all the good we tried to do, we only seemed to make things worse. And *we* ended up in a mess. We started to hate both our parents and at the same time felt guilty knowing that we should love them. Alateen takes away our need to referee and shows us how to detach. We learn to let go of our parents' problems and let *them* take care of the trouble that comes between them. This gives us more time to work on our own problems, especially our guilt feelings and the walls we've built between ourselves and our parents.

Things to Think About

I get involved in my parents' problems because I think I can help. The program has a message for me: DETACH. When I let my parents "fight it out" between themselves without getting involved, I find I've got lots of time and energy left over to love them when the fighting is done.

Living with an alcoholic left me feeling lost, scared, confused, and bitter. I hated myself and blamed the whole world. I just couldn't cope anymore.

I came to Alateen as a last hope. The members guided me to a new way of life. They shared their experiences with me and showed me the way to live with myself. I also learned to detach from the people I love and live my own life instead of getting wrapped up in theirs.

Today I'm very grateful for the program and the people in it. They've shown me the way to find happiness in each day and thanks to them, I'm learning to like myself again.

Things to Think About

Alateens understand because they've been there. They know what it's like to be hurt, humiliated, afraid, and ashamed. But they also know the joy of putting their lives back together. I'm thankful for the tools they've given me to work with. Today I'll try to make a special effort to use them.

When I was little and I fell and hurt myself, my mother would always put a band-aid on my cut and tell me the hurt would go away. It usually did. As I grew older and started to have problems in my life, I depended on my mother to use her "band-aids" to make the hurt go away again. She protected me and told me everything would be okay. For a time it seemed she was right, but the hurt always kept coming back.

In Alateen I learned that my mother's "band-aid solutions" to my problems wouldn't work. They only covered over what was really wrong inside of me. When I began to apply the program, I took a good, long look at myself. That's when I finally started to get to the bottom of what was making me hurt so bad. Once I found that out, it was a lot easier to do something *for myself* to make the hurt go away.

Things to Think About

There are still times when I hurt inside. Other people can make me feel good for awhile, but I have to do something for myself if I really want to get rid of the pain. Putting the program to work in my life is a way of doing just that. It helps me find where it hurts so I can start getting better.

I'd been in the program awhile before my mother stopped drinking. Afterward, I began wondering if I still needed Alateen. Could I still help others and could they help me even though the alcoholic wasn't drinking anymore?

I took another look at the "Do You Need Alateen?" questions in my Alateen book and I answered "Yes" to a lot of them. This helped me to realize that what I get out of Alateen depends on me, not the condition of the alcoholic.

I need the program more than ever today. In fact, I wouldn't think of living my life without it. It makes my life more manageable.

Things to Think About

Alateen is a way of life for me. It has nothing to do with whether the alcoholic is sober or drinking. Do I need it? Yes! if I want to learn how to live with myself.

Before Alateen, when I made plans for things, I used to plan the results, too. If I was planning to go to a dance, I was sure it would be terrific; if I was studying for a test, I knew I'd pass with no trouble at all. How could things go wrong with me at the controls?

When my planned results flopped, I'd feel miserable and resentful; I was a failure! Sometimes I even looked for someone else to blame.

I still make plans today, but I'm learning to "Let Go and Let God." I do the groundwork and He takes care of the end results. Things have a way of working out a lot better that way!

Things to Think About

It's okay to make plans, but the results are out of my hands. When I try to fix the way things turn out, I may be asking to be let down. If I let go and leave the results up to my Higher Power, He'll take care of things better than I ever could.

Alcoholism is serious business. But does that mean we have to walk around looking as if we're carrying the world on our shoulders? Some of us thought so—until we came to Alateen.

At my first meeting I was surprised to find so many people laughing about things that I'd always taken so seriously. "You don't laugh about things like this," I thought.

But, in a strange way, the laughter kept bringing me back. It almost seemed as if it took away some of the hurt and helped to shrink my problems down to a size that's easier to handle.

It was contagious, too. In time *I* started to laugh at things I'd done and said—things that used to be earth-shattering. And did it ever feel good!

Things to Think About

Someone once said that finding the humor in a problem can be the beginning of solving it. As I stick with Alateen, I learn to laugh at myself. Today I'll find something to laugh about and try to take life just a little less seriously.

It takes courage to be independent. It's a lot easier to follow the crowd and it's usually more fun. Being Mr. Clean or Miss Goodie-Two-Shoes isn't a very popular way to be.

But following the crowd can get me into things that mess up my life. It takes courage to "be myself" and not to do what everyone else is doing.

Alateen has helped me to find that kind of courage. I believe in myself and I'm learning to stick with the winners.

Things to Think About

I've decided to follow the path of the Alateens before me. They're the ones I want to be like. Following their lead and knowing that I'm in charge of myself has helped me to bridge the gap between what I used to be like and the person I want to be.

My father spoiled what could have been happy times in our family. He wasted the money we needed for important things like food and clothes. He didn't show any interest in what I was doing and when I really needed to talk to him, he wasn't there.

The program helped me to understand that my father was suffering from a disease. That explained a lot of his behavior, but I still found it hard to forgive him for what he'd done. I wanted to get back at him and show him how much he'd hurt me. But nothing I did ever got through to him; it just left me feeling chewed up inside.

In time I learned to be less critical of him; I tried to be more patient and understanding. With the help of the Steps, I decided to let go of the past. It felt as if a big weight had been lifted off my shoulders. I was free to concentrate on working *my* program for *myself.*

Things to Think About

Sometimes I want to get even with the alcoholic for everything he's done to me. It feels good until I realize that I'm really only punishing myself. When I ease off and try to understand the alcoholic instead of condemning him, I feel a lot better and it helps me keep my focus where it belongs: on my own recovery.

I used to have trouble with the slogan "Think." Some Alateens say it really helps them to think things through carefully before they start to do something important. It helped me, too. But it got to be a problem.

I used to think so much that I'd never do anything else. I had to take everything apart and examine all the details, almost like I was looking at a bug under a microscope. By the time I'd thought about everything, I didn't have the energy left to *do* anything.

Then I learned that taking so long to think about things was really just another form of procrastination. I started to use some of the other slogans to stop procrastinating. "Easy Does It" and "Let Go and Let God" helped me to relax, let go of my need to look at everything in such detail, and have the faith and courage to move ahead into action.

Now I try to think carefully, but not so much that I forget about the "doing."

Things to Think About

I have to think about things, but thinking too much can really hurt me; it's a way to keep from doing anything. Instead of spending all my time thinking about what to do, I'll try to stop procrastinating and put my thinking into action.

When my mother told me I had to go to Alateen, I said, "No way! That's not for me! I have a happy life without it and I'm not affected by the disease anyway." That wasn't true and I knew it. I just needed an excuse to stay home.

My mother took me to my first meeting. Forcefully, I might add. But after that first meeting, I needed no more persuading. Alateen and I hit it off right away. The smiles and laughter made me feel comfortable and the way people opened up made me feel as if I could really trust them.

I go to meetings now because *I* want to. It's helping me to become a better person. There are times when I don't feel like going, but when I think about all that the program has given me, I know I'm doing the right thing.

Things to Think About

I used to make excuses to stay away from Alateen. Now I'm glad I got here, even if I was forced to come. I have a lot of new friends and I have a chance to do something positive about my life. If I'm ever tempted to think about staying away again, remembering how much the program has done for me will help me change my mind.

Alateen members kept telling me that alcoholism is a disease that affects the whole family. At first I wouldn't believe them because my mother was the only one who was drinking. But the more I thought about the way things were at home, the more I understood what they meant.

My mother's drinking made her mean and irritable. She yelled and screamed at us even when we didn't do anything. Everybody was uptight and miserable. Although I was coming apart inside I never told my mother how I felt. I just let her have her own way to try to keep peace in the house.

That's when I finally realized how sick *I* had become. It scared me and I wanted to do something about it. My Alateen friends guided me to Step One. By working on it, I started to accept alcoholism as a *family* disease and in time, I found the courage to express my real feelings.

Things to Think About

It's not difficult to understand why alcoholism is called a family disease. Sometimes I feel handcuffed to the alcoholic. Her moods are my moods, her reactions are my reactions, her illness is my illness. But now I have something that helps me to break away—the Twelve Step program. If I use it every day, I can recover and find a better way of life for me.

In Alateen we find people who are just like us. *We're equals.* There are no teachers—just learners who are trying to make better lives for themselves by sharing their experience, strength, and hope with each other.

We need one another. We lean on each other until we're strong enough to stand. Then we let others lean on us. What we can't do alone, we can do together. That's how the program works!

Things to Think About

I'm part of a fellowship of people helping people. Knowing that makes it a lot easier for me to reach out to others and say, "I can't do it alone." Together *we* can make it!

I once heard a song about a person who missed seeing a beautiful rainbow because she spent so much time looking at the cracks in the sidewalk. It reminded me of my own life. The cracks were like my problems, and the rainbow all the good things around me.

Naturally, I have to be prepared to face my problems, but when I do nothing but stare at them, I cheat myself out of all the special things that are there for the taking every day. How do I stop staring at the "cracks in the sidewalk?" I use the Serenity Prayer and Steps Three to Seven to turn my problems over to my Higher Power and ask for the courage to start doing something to get rid of them. That helps me to "look up" and really enjoy all the good things in my life each day.

Things to Think About

My problems can get me down if I don't have something or someone to help pick me up. Thanks to the program I have a Higher Power who's ready to give me a hand. When I'm willing to tackle my problems with His help, I'll be able to see more of the bright spots in my life.

Life is more fun if I have a positive attitude. When I get rid of words like "can't," "won't," and "don't want to" and replace them with "can," "will," and "I'll give it a try," things go more smoothly for me and I get a lot more done. If I look for the good in something instead of the bad, I'm much happier. And if I smile and say a kind word to someone, instead of frowning and growling, people seem to want to be with me and that makes my day more enjoyable.

Some days, though, all this seems like an impossible thing to do, especially when everything I do turns out wrong. But having a positive attitude works like a music lesson: the more I practice it, the easier it becomes. If I'm willing to give it a chance, I may find myself looking at a brighter today.

Things to Think About

Think positive! That's easier said than done, particularly on days when things are really getting me down. But I'll never know what a positive attitude feels like unless I try it. If I take the time to be a more positive person today, I might be surprised by all the good I'll see around me.

My life used to center around my alcoholic parent. If he was sober, I was happy. If he was drinking, I was depressed and angry and passed that mood on to others. I also felt responsible for my younger brothers and sisters, and constantly nagged them, but the end result was my own frustration.

The First Step in the program has changed all that for me. I've admitted that I'm powerless. I know that my alcoholic parent is sick and realize that it's the illness I hate, not him. I no longer have to let that illness rule my life. Now that I recognize it, I can detach with love and let my anger and hate disappear.

Things to Think About

Through the program I'm learning to forget about the past and make the most of each day. Detachment is one of the keys. It means living my own life as well as I can and letting others live theirs. By practicing detachment, I can learn to accept and love myself again and pass that acceptance and love on to others.

Before Alateen I used my family to cover for my wrongs. I was always ready to jump at everyone for all the things that didn't meet my approval. When things weren't right in our home, I was quick to put all the blame on my parents, brothers, and sisters.

Then I heard at an Alateen meeting that when you point a finger at someone, there are three pointing back at yourself. I wondered if I might be a little bit wrong in the way I'd judged my family.

Today I'm learning to stop shifting the blame to other people. I'm starting to accept responsibility for my own actions. I'm a lot happier and so is my family.

Things to Think About

It's a sign of real growth when I stop blaming other people for my "bad luck" and start doing my part to make things better. The program has the tools to help me do this. It's up to me to use them.

Alateen isn't just a place to unburden my troubles and feel sorry for myself. Sometimes when I complain too much about my troubles, it makes them seem bigger and they get a real hold on me.

I need the chance to share my feelings, but I need a sense of direction, too. That's why I use the Steps and work the program. By listening to others discuss how they handle their feelings, and by talking openly about my feelings, I can break the hold self-pity has on my life.

Alateen gives me two choices: I can hold on to my self-pity or work it out with the help of the program and my Alateen friends. If I want to grow, the choice is simple.

Things to Think About

Before Alateen I resented everything in my life. I thought I was the only one who was suffering and I was always asking, "Why me?" Through the program I learned to be honest with myself and to give myself a chance to see the good things in life. Today, instead of feeling sorry for myself, I'll be able to look at the positive side of things and be good to myself.

I used to be a very ungrateful person. I asked a lot of my Higher Power and when I got help, I took it for granted and never said "thank you." I thought that was what He was there for.

Step Seven helped me change my thinking. Now that I firmly believe in my Higher Power, I've found that things are working out much better. I'm still asking for His help because each day there are things I need to deal with: a small argument, a problem at school, something in Alateen. But now I humbly ask Him for help and don't just expect things to work out the way I want them to. I know they'll work out the way that's best for me.

Things to Think About

Being humble simply means being honest. I can't get rid of my shortcomings by myself. My Higher Power will help me; all I have to do is ask.

Sometimes I think I've got the program and I know what I want. But I have to be careful that what I want doesn't turn into trying to control other people. It's easy to start thinking I have all the right answers and expect others to do things my way. I can even get mad at people for not doing what *I* think is right.

But Step One means concentrating on myself, not trying to control others. The Serenity Prayer tells me to "accept the things I cannot change." That means accepting others for what they are, not what I want them to be. If I put myself in their place and try to understand their feelings, it helps me get my bearings again. I can stop trying to control others, accept them, and get back to working my program.

Things to Think About

When I try to control someone, it keeps me from taking care of *my* life. If people act in a way that's different from the way I do things, that's their business. I don't have to offer an opinion unless I'm asked. Allowing others to speak and act for themselves is a kind of acceptance that helps me mind my own business. I have my own things to do today. I'll spend my time thinking about them.

In Alateen we're all searching for recovery. It's like following a road. Along the way we meet special friends who understand us and we join with them and walk together.

Sometimes we stumble while we're traveling. But our friends are there to help us get back up and straighten ourselves out. Even if we leave the road for a while, they'll wait patiently for us to come back and walk with them again.

Recovery means something different to each of us, but it's good to know we can walk together. If we're patient, we'll find what we're looking for.

Things to Think About

I've been affected by alcoholism and I need to recover. Alateen gives me the chance to walk the road of recovery with other people who want to get better. Just knowing we're in it together makes it easier to move ahead with hope.

I believe my Higher Power has given me talents to use. I try to be grateful for them, but sometimes my attitude is a real obstacle. I compare myself to other people and think they're better than I am.

The program shows me that comparing myself to others is an easy way to make excuses for not using what I have. If I take an honest look around, I'll see a lot of opportunities to use my abilities, in and out of the fellowship. Doing things to help others is one good way. It's a kind of service that reminds me to thank my Higher Power for the talents I've been given and for the growth which takes place when I use them.

Things to Think About

I have some special abilities. They're like gifts from my Higher Power. But I have to do my part and use them. Helping people will put them to good use and show my Higher Power how grateful I am.

Flowers need sunshine *and* rain to grow and blossom. If they only have sunshine, they wither and die.

It's like that with life, too. I have to take the rain along with the sunshine. Sometimes I wish I didn't have any problems. But without them my life might be boring and I'd miss out on some great opportunities to grow.

Growth can be very painful, but the problems I have can make me dig deep to find answers. They help me form roots in the program. They make me a stronger person and keep me growing each day.

Things to Think About

I don't like the obstacles in my life, but often they help make me a stronger person. With the help of the program, I won't be afraid to face my problems today. They'll help me grow and blossom into a better person.

Silence is good for me, especially when I'm tense and upset. I get away from everybody and spend time by myself being peaceful. The quiet time really helps to "calm the rough waters" inside me.

But if I'm not careful, I can use silence as a weapon, too. Sometimes, when people get on my nerves, I give them the silent treatment to let them know I don't want to have anything to do with them. There's nothing peaceful about it. This kind of silence is meant to hurt and it does, both the other person and me.

How I use silence is up to me. But if I'm really interested in helping myself, the choice is simple. Silence can be just what I need to get in touch with myself and find some peace of mind today.

Things to Think About

Silence talks. It can scream out in anger or it can be a calm and gentle whisper inside me. If I'm looking for some quiet time today, I'll tune out the screams and start listening to the whispers.

Trying to do God's will is like walking down a path and coming to a patch of strawberries that stretches as far as we can see. We know we should stay on the main path, but we really like strawberries. For a moment we don't know what to do. Then we start wandering through the patch, telling ourselves we'll only taste a few. But we keep picking strawberries until we get so far from the path that we're lost and we're sure there's no hope of finding our way back again.

When we do things our way and get ourselves into trouble, we think God will never take us back again. But He will, if we're willing to try. With the help of Alateen, we can find our way back to the main path.

Things to Think About

It's hard to know what God's will is for me. It's even harder to carry it out. Sometimes I get sidetracked and want to do things my own way, but it never seems to work out. Step Eleven can help. If I stay in touch with my Higher Power and ask for His help, He'll let me know what He thinks is best for me and He'll give me the strength to do it.

I was quick-tempered and moody. If I didn't get my own way, I'd go off in a huff and refuse to speak to anybody. Or if people said something nasty about me, I'd snap at them, then leave, thinking everybody hated me.

The program is helping me to be a little less self-centered. I don't sulk as much as I used to and if I don't get my own way, it's probably for the best. If people say things that aren't so nice, I don't fly off the handle the way I did before. I try to remember that's their opinion and let it go.

Things to Think About

Sometimes I think the whole world revolves around me, but the program is there to remind me that it doesn't. When people don't treat me the way I want to be treated or do things the way I think they should be done, I'll remember that everybody is entitled to their opinion. I know what I believe about myself. I'll use the program today to be comfortable with that.

An important thing in our group is that everyone is involved. Responsibilities are shared so that all members are able to feel a part of the group. Everybody gives up a bit of their time to help out. It's one of the ways we practice the Seventh Tradition.

But we have to support our group by giving our money as well. Some of us can't donate anything when we first come; some of us still can't give very much; we give as much as we can afford.

Practicing Tradition Seven is a good way to go. The result is we all have the rewarding feeling that we're helping to keep our group going.

Things to Think About

I can support my group in a number of ways. When the basket is passed, I can give whatever I can. Just as important, I can give my time and moral support to help make ours the kind of group I *want* to belong to.

When my serenity is low, I overreact to everything around me. A quick Tenth Step inventory tells me I'm letting things get out of perspective; I'm losing control.

Once I recognize the problem, I can start to work on it. I use the Serenity Prayer to help me regain control of my emotions. Then I ask myself, "Why did I overreact?" When I find some answers to that question, I make amends to myself and other people and try to make changes so it doesn't happen again.

Things to Think About

Sometimes I let my emotions get out of hand. I hurt a lot of people, including myself, when I overreact. The program has something to calm me down: the Serenity Prayer. I'll use it today when I feel my self-control slipping away.

I used to bring my friends home to watch TV or play a game. As soon as we'd come through the door, I would smell the booze. I'd be embarrassed to see the shape my parents were in and so would my friends. Eventually, I couldn't stand it anymore and stopped having them over.

The program helped me to understand that my parents are sick. I learned not to be embarrassed or ashamed of their drinking because they have a disease called alcoholism.

I'm feeling more comfortable now and I've started asking my friends over again. When I invite them, I tell them about our family situation and how I feel about it. Most of them can accept it; some can't. That's okay because I couldn't at one time either. What's important to me now is that I can accept my parents as they are.

Things to Think About

Alcoholism is a disease not a disgrace. Thanks to all I'm learning in Alateen, I believe that now. I'm not embarrassed by my parents anymore because I know they are sick. That makes it a lot easier on my friends. Not all of them can accept the situation, but that doesn't matter. *I* do and I feel comfortable today.

I used to resent it whenever our group had a "bad" meeting. I thought if they really cared about me, they wouldn't fool around or come to the meeting unprepared. Sometimes, I'd get so upset that I'd sit in a corner and sulk, not taking part in the meeting.

One night, on the way home from a meeting like this, my Sponsor and I talked. He asked if I was looking for bad things to happen to give me an excuse to feel sorry for myself. That made me stop and think. I realized then that *I* was most of the problem. How could I get anything out of the meetings if I was so wrapped up in self-pity?

Now I remind myself that whenever I resent anything, I'm the one who misses out. If a meeting doesn't go well, I speak up and try to put in my share to get it back on track. I get a lot out of most of our meetings now; I wonder if it has anything to do with my change of attitude.

Things to Think About

When things don't go as well as I expect at a meeting, I can mope around and feel sorry for myself. But it won't get me very far. Instead, I can get involved. It might make a difference to what someone else gets out of the meeting and it definitely will make a difference to me.

I can manipulate myself in many ways. Sometimes I don't feel like studying for a test, so I convince myself that I'll likely not pass the test anyway. That kind of attitude gives me an excuse for not studying, but it usually ends up hurting me. I dwell on failing the test for so long that it really does happen.

In Alateen I learn to change the attitudes that hurt me. There are a lot of things I don't want to do, but making excuses for my actions is just a way of avoiding responsibility. If I can make an effort to pass (even if it means studying), I'll learn a lot about facing my problems and that's a big step toward being responsible.

Things to Think About

I can avoid anything I don't want to do just by thinking up an excuse. The program shows me that's a good way to cheat myself. Instead I'll use the program today to change my thinking and face up to the responsibilities I've been trying to avoid for a long time.

When I was worked up about my problems at home, anything would set me off. If someone looked at me the wrong way or said something I didn't want to hear, I'd blow up. People at school bothered me the most and I took out my frustrations by beating them up.

Things are starting to change now that I'm in Alateen. I'm learning to cope with the people at school. I realize now that my frustrations are *inside of me* and have nothing to do with anyone else. I'm starting to work out those feelings by talking to my friends and using slogans like "Easy Does It." I have better control of my temper now. In fact, I haven't hit anyone in quite a while! Even my schoolwork is improving. I'm making good progress and it's all because of the program.

Things to Think About

When I lose my temper, I'm out of control and innocent people end up getting hurt. The program helps me find control again. When I start to understand my problems better, I can learn how to let go of a lot of my frustration. Today, when I feel things starting to boil over inside of me, I'll remember "Easy Does It" and practice a bit of self-control.

I used to think God was just a noun, a word
that didn't mean much to me. As time went by,
I learned to be afraid of that word because I was
sure God was ready to punish me for everything I
did wrong.

Now, because of the program, I think of God
as something real. He's understanding and caring.
He's the verb "to love" and every action that goes
with it.

I can be a part of His "love in action." When I
help a newcomer see a different point of view or
when I take time to listen to someone who wants
to talk, I get to know about the special kind of love
that makes our fellowship what it is.

Things to Think About

There's a Power in every meeting I attend. Some
call it God, others call it Love. To me, it's the same
thing. I reach out to others and they reach out to
me. Together we put the love into action that keeps
us all alive.

After I came to Alateen I realized that my parents were sick. I used to hate them, but when I started to understand they were suffering from the disease of alcoholism, I had a lot more love for them.

In Alateen I've learned that drinking is their problem, not mine. I can't stop it; it's a choice *they* have to make.

Each day I try to remember to "Live and Let Live." Instead of living my parents' lives and taking on their responsibilities, I take care of me.

Things to Think About

Today I'll live my own life and let others live theirs. I won't be discouraged by what anyone says or does and I won't be influenced by others around me. I'll be my own person.

I need to keep my own thinking straight if I want to help people. I have to make sure I know the difference between responding to others and taking responsibility for them.

When someone asks me for help, I can carry the message to the person, but I don't have to carry the person to the message. I can try to listen to what the person has to say and share what the program has done for me. But then I have to give some time and space and let the person move in his own way. That shows him the respect he's entitled to and keeps me strong and healthy.

Things to Think About

Sometimes I get so excited about reaching out to other people that I forget what helping really means. If I'm trying to carry people instead of the message of the program, I could be hurting a lot of people, including me. But if I let people know that I care, and back off and let them do things in their own time, I'll be helping them find some respect for themselves and maintaining my self-respect, too.

At first I came to Alateen just to get out of the house. I was tired of sitting around and I thought it would be a good excuse to be with people my own age. I never missed a meeting, but I was never really "there." I fooled around and never listened to what people were saying. I went mostly to talk and have a good time.

Then one night the Group Chairman asked everybody to say a few words about why we were coming to Alateen. I was stuck. I couldn't tell the truth so I made up some things I thought would sound good. I didn't believe a word I said and I don't think anyone else did either. That night I went home and thought for a long time about why I was going to Alateen.

I came back the next week because I wanted to. I listened and decided to let the program be my way of life. I started to work at the Steps and tried to make them a part of everything I was doing.

Things to Think About

Alateen isn't just a place to go every week. It's a meeting that offers me a new way of life. It has answers for me, but I have to be willing to look for them.

When I started in Alateen, I couldn't see much to be grateful for. My main thought was: "If people only treated me better, everything would be okay." I spent a lot of time daydreaming and feeling sorry for myself. I didn't realize how big a part attitudes played in my life.

As I watched the growth of my friends in the program, I became aware of a different way of living. I saw their happiness and I wanted it, too. My first step toward finding it was to apply a new thought from Al-Anon literature. "Just for today I will be happy; most folks are as happy as they make up their minds to be."

This was a new beginning for me. I started to realize that my happiness depended on me, not on others. I made an effort to be happy and after a lot of practice it became a habit.

Things to Think About

If I'm unhappy and looking for people to blame, it's time I looked at my own attitude. I am responsible for my own happiness. If I try to use the program ideas in my life, I can be as happy as I make up my mind to be today.

It's hard living without one parent. My father left our family when my parents were divorced. I was very young and I couldn't understand why my father didn't stay with us the way my friends' fathers did. Whenever my father did come back, he was usually drunk and I'd run away and hide because I was afraid of him.

When I was older, I went to Alateen. I didn't like it at first; it reminded me of all my bad feelings about our family. But after awhile, I started to make friends with some of the people. Like me, many of them had only one parent and as I listened to them talk about their feelings, I felt more comfortable. They helped me to understand that while the program wouldn't change the fact of my parents' divorce, it could help me to do something about myself if I'd let it. That made me want to stay around and let the program work for me.

Things to Think About

Alateen can't "fix" my family situation, but it can help me to change my attitude toward it. Instead of wishing that things were different, I can accept that things are the way they are and get on with working on my own problems. That's where the program will help me the most if I give it a chance today.

When I hear the word "unity," it makes me think about the First Tradition. It's the bond that draws our group together as the members share their experience, strength, and hope with each other.

But unity really starts within me. I think of it as a feeling of "getting things together" inside my own head. I can think more clearly now and my feelings aren't as scrambled as they used to be. I can even make a few decisions for myself.

Unity comes from working the Twelve Steps in my life each day, helping me feel like a whole person again. Because I'm in better shape today than I've ever been, I have a lot more to offer to my group and the fellowship as a whole.

Things to Think About

I don't feel as if I'm falling apart anymore. Working the program is helping me to put my life back together. It's a good feeling—a "unity" inside myself—that gives me a chance to lend some solid support to the fellowship that's helped me "pick up the pieces" in my life.

My friends in Alateen are willing to help me if I let them. If I share a bit of myself with them, I can get close to them and let them get to know me.

I don't have to be afraid to talk to them because they've gone through the same things as I have. They take the time to sit down and listen to what I have to say and then they let me know how they've handled their problems. Sometimes one of them says something I don't want to hear, but I don't have to take it hard because I know they're just trying to help me.

I trust my friends. What we say to each other stays with us. Nobody goes out and talks about what's been said. Knowing that has helped me most of all. At last I can say how I really feel and know that somebody wants to listen and help me.

Things to Think About

Alateens are special friends. They make it easy for me to talk about myself because they're willing to listen and share their own feelings with me. I trust them with my life. When I need help, I know they're always there.

When the alcoholic was drinking, I was constantly asking, "Why me?" I was ashamed and felt like my whole world was in pieces.

Now, bit-by-bit, my life is being built up again. The program is shaping me like a sculptor who is creating a new figure. I've taken Step One and admitted that I'm powerless over alcohol and I'm learning to "Live and Let Live." I know I can't change an alcoholic or anyone else.

I have my own life to live and I want to live it to the fullest. With the help of the program I'll be able to get as much out of each day as I can.

Things to Think About

I feel like a different person today—whole and new. I'm free from self-pity and I can carry my head high wherever I go. It feels great and I want to keep it that way. The program will show me how, if I'm willing to live it each day.

What's so important about being right? Why do I fight with my parents when I know it's only going to make things worse? Our whole family is sick because of living with alcoholism. We don't need any more problems.

I have to learn to stop arguing. Instead of fighting everything my parents say, I need to respect their point of view, whether it makes sense to me or not.

Using slogans is a big help. "Easy Does It" helps me shut my mouth and open my ears: "Live and Let Live" reminds me that my parents have a right to their feelings, too; and "Let Go and Let God" shows me how to detach and let my Higher Power take care of our family. Together, slogans are a good way to stop an explosion before it gets started.

Things to Think About

I have to stand up for what I believe, but I'm not always right. Fighting about it doesn't get our family anywhere. We have enough problems already without my causing more. The slogans have some answers for me. When I use them, I get a better picture of what's happening to our family and I can do my part to make our home a more peaceful place to live.

"Alcoholic" used to be a dirty word to me. I grew up with a negative attitude toward alcoholism and alcoholics. That attitude stayed with me into my teenage years. When my sister developed a drinking problem, I reacted in my usual manner by calling her a bad person and the "black sheep" of the family.

Some time later my mother joined Al-Anon and my sister went to A.A.. I saw a new bond growing between them and was jealous, so I started going to Al-Anon to be a part of things. In Al-Anon I-found out about Alateen and decided to give it a try.

I've started working on myself now and I've changed my attitude toward my sister and her illness. I'm trying to be more understanding and I think the bond between us is getting stronger all the time.

Things to Think About

Holding on to my negative ideas about alcoholism can keep me from understanding what's really going on in our family. The program can open up some new doors in my mind if I let it. It can help me change some of my old attitudes so I can enjoy a better relationship with my family and others today.

I have one mouth and two ears. The reason for that should have been obvious to me, but before coming to the fellowship I acted as if I had two mouths and one ear. I talked and talked and hardly ever listened to anything other people had to say.

The program has helped me to set my priorities straight. Step Four helped me to recognize that I talked a lot to cover up my own insecure feelings. I guess I felt if I talked enough, something I said would make sense and someone would listen to me.

Step Eleven helped me to be a better listener. Silence was hard for me to handle at first because I'd always thought I needed to fill it up with my own voice. Practicing prayer and meditation showed me how to use the quiet time to listen to my Higher Power's guidance. As I started to do more of it, I found it easier to listen to people as well, and I realized how much there was to gain by doing more listening than talking.

Things to Think About

There are times for talking and times for listening. The program helps me to sort out which is which. By using the Steps, I can learn to put my ears and mouth to good use and get a lot more out of my conversations with others.

Before coming to Alateen, I alternated between being afraid and pretending to be brave and fearless. Sometimes I was afraid of specific things, but I covered it up; sometimes I didn't even know what I was afraid of and I spent my time running scared; and sometimes I was simply afraid to be afraid. Living like this wasn't living at all!

Today I can admit that I'm afraid. There's nothing wrong with that. I'm learning to identify my fears and face them. It might be fear of failure—at school, as a friend, or as a son or daughter; or maybe it's a fear of showing my feelings. It doesn't matter. Listening at meetings helps me to realize that a lot of other people have the same kinds of fears as I do. Working the program gives us the chance to overcome them together.

Things to Think About

"I'm afraid!" Admitting that is the first step to overcoming my fears. Sharing with the other members helps me to put my finger on the things I'm afraid of and gives me tools and understanding friends to help me work on getting rid of my fears.

Sometimes we become so upset with the bad things that happen to us that we're blinded by our anger. We don't take time to see the good in things that have happened. We blame God and other people for our problems and refuse to learn from our mistakes.

In Alateen we learn to take responsibility for our own actions. We try to accept what is and see the good in it. Sometimes that takes real courage. But we know now that God can help us calm down, and get a better perspective on things so we can learn something valuable from every situation.

Things to Think About

Instead of blaming God and the people close to us for everything that goes wrong today, I'll take a look at my own attitude. I'll try to keep an open mind and see the good in situations so I can learn something about myself in everything that happens to me today.

There are three persons I have to admit my shortcomings to in Step Five: God, myself, and another human being. The order is no coincidence for me. My Higher Power is the easiest for me to admit my faults to. I know He's always there, ready to listen to me and forgive me. But the second person is more difficult. The "me" inside never wants to accept that anything can be wrong with me. Admitting what I'm really like helps me overcome this problem and find some humility.

The hardest thing is admitting my faults to another person. No matter how much courage I have, I seem to lose it out of fear of what that other person might think of me. But when I talk about my faults and the reasons behind them, it's a chance to build up trust between the two of us.

No matter how hard it is to do Step Five, it's a relief to get rid of the many feelings I've hidden from everyone, including myself. It's like finding a special kind of freedom.

Things to Think About

Admitting my defects to God, to myself, and to another person gives me an honest picture of who I am. That starts me on the road to true humility.

Admitting my wrongs to another person is a start to overcoming them. But I have to go further than that. I have to be ready to have them removed, and Step Six shows me how.

To become ready, I don't have to run around looking for ways to get rid of my defects. I just have to be willing to let my Higher Power help me. If I'm open, He'll show me the way.

I don't expect to be perfect, but I know I'll start to improve if I show an honest desire to ask God to help me with my faults. That will help me to get ready to work on them, "One Day at a Time," until they're removed.

Things To Think About

God can't help me until I'm ready. That's the key to Step Six. If I'm still hanging on to my favorite faults, I'm hurting my chances for serenity. But if I'm willing to let go, God will help me with the rest.

When I lived with an alcoholic, I shut out a lot of the people around me. I was so tied up in my own problems that I didn't listen to anyone else and I thought no one was listening to me.

When I came to Alateen I found a group of friends who *were* willing to listen. They made me feel welcome and comfortable because they cared enough to listen to what I was saying. They even seemed to be able to hear the things I wasn't saying in words.

The more they listened to me, the more my Alateen friends helped me to listen to them. In time, I realized that listening to others helped me to get the most out of the program. I learned a lot about handling my problems. It gave me a chance to help others do the same.

Things to Think About

The slogan "Listen and Learn" makes sense when I put it into action. People who listen to others seem to learn the most about putting the program to work in their lives. If I can get my mind off my own problems and really listen to other people, I'll learn a lot more today about the good things Alateen has to offer me.

Do I have the courage to face the problems that alcoholism has brought into my life? Can I knock down the wall of loneliness that I've been building?

The answer could be "yes," if I'd stop hiding behind my wall when something happens that I don't like. When I withdraw, I make myself even more unhappy because I shut in my bad feelings and I shut out other people.

In Alateen, people understand how I feel. Most of them have lived behind walls, too. I can share my fears and hurts with them. They help me to take down my wall and start building a bridge to a world of courage and peace of mind.

Things to Think About

It's easy to hide behind a wall instead of facing my problems, but I'm the one who loses when I do. I close myself in and other people can't reach me. The program helps me to break through my wall and build a bridge to a new way of life.

When I'm having a bad day and I see the alcoholic drinking, I want to say something. But I realize I'll only get myself upset. The alcoholic has a habit of saying things he doesn't mean and sometimes his words make me feel unwanted and insecure.

What can I do? I can try to detach. When the alcoholic says something that hurts me, I let the comments bounce off of me. Then I try to find a quiet place where I can be by myself for awhile. I read some Al-Anon/Alateen literature, think things through, and talk with my Higher Power. Later I call an Alateen friend and let my feelings out.

Things to Think About

The program gives me the choice of whether or not to become involved in the alcoholic's life. I can avoid a lot of bad scenes by learning to detach. If I feel myself reacting to the alcoholic today, I'll try to let go, calm down, and get a better grip on my feelings.

Sometimes I go on ego trips. I'm the center of attention and I think I have it made. I'm sure I can make it on my own and don't need the program anymore. Then I get into trouble and realize I do need help and can't do it alone.

This help can come from my Higher Power. Step Seven reminds me to humbly ask Him for it. Sometimes I take my Higher Power for granted. But I know, if it wasn't for the love, understanding, and patience I receive, I wouldn't have the life I have today. That's something I never want to forget.

Things to Think About

When I need someone to put my life back together, God is there. But I have to ask Him to help me. My way of thanking my Higher Power for help is to keep working the program the best way I can.

I came to Alateen when I was down and feeling rotten. So many unkind and untrue things had been said about me that I started to believe them.

The people in my Alateen group were different; they listened and they cared. They saw good in me and helped me to recognize it in myself. They reminded me that as long as God and I know what's true about me, that's all that really matters. They helped me most by showing me how to work the Steps. That gave me the chance to believe in myself and to keep building on the good things inside of me.

Today I realize that I *am* someone. I treat myself like the good friend my fellow Alateens tell me I am. Even if people say things and I feel hurt or disappointed, I don't have to let them pull me down. I can try to be happy and remember that no one can take away my good feeling about myself.

Things to Think About

Many of us don't come to believe in ourselves until somebody points out what's good in us. That's what my Alateen friends do for me by sharing how they live the Twelve Steps. Today I don't have to depend on anyone for my good feeling. It's inside of me and I can see it clearly because I'm trying to live the program.

Sometimes we try to cover up our true feelings. Maybe we're afraid of what our life at home may bring, or angry about the way other people treat us. Maybe we feel awkward and inferior around our friends, or frustrated with the work and teachers at school. But instead of showing these feelings to the people around us, we put on an act and pretend that everything is fine.

Feelings are a part of us; we can't control them. But we *can* control what we do with them. That's where the program can help. It gives us the chance to talk honestly about our feelings, to do something positive about them.

Things to Think About

For a long time I wore a mask to convince everybody that I was feeling fine when I was really coming apart inside. Today I'll try to be honest about how I feel. I'll work out my feelings in ways that are good for me and let other people get to know the real me.

I don't think anyone can say they've never hurt anyone. We all make mistakes because we're not perfect.

The person I hurt the most was me. For a long time I felt sorry for myself. The worry, fear, hate, and shame I felt about my family made me insecure. I had no self-confidence and I couldn't accept myself.

After taking a good look at myself, I realize now I have to put me on my list of amends. I have to be willing to apologize to myself if I want to put my past behind me and continue growing in the program.

Things To Think About

If I've really let myself go downhill, Step Eight will help me turn things around. Instead of feeling sorry for myself, I can get ready to say, "I'm sorry!" by being willing to be good to myself and others.

When I first came to meetings, Alateen was just a place to pass the time. It didn't mean anything to me.

After realizing that I wasn't getting anything out of the program, I started to work the Steps. I began to understand some of the Alateen ideas. I gained a lot of new trusting friends and I found answers to many of my questions.

Now that I realize my responsibility to myself, I'm trying to make better use of my time. I'm getting a lot more out of the program and I'm enjoying life the way I've always wanted to.

Things to Think About

Today I have twenty-four hours to live. I can waste the time or use it wisely, trying to work the program in everything I do. The choice is mine.

Once there was an Alateen member who went to meetings regularly. He enjoyed them, but in recent weeks, they seemed to be missing what he really needed. He knew it wasn't the meetings; the time had come for him to make a choice—quit or move on to Al-Anon.

He didn't want to quit the program and give up everything that meant so much to him, but at the same time, he was afraid to move on. It seemed like a gigantic step into the unknown. What if he didn't know enough about the program? What if he made everybody feel uncomfortable? What if they didn't want him?

Finally he decided to give it a try. At first he felt a bit awkward, but there was such a good feeling in the room that he realized Al-Anon wasn't that different from Alateen. As he relaxed and let the other members help him, he realized that Al-Anon is really just another step in working the program.

Things to Think About

It's good to know that Al-Anon is there when the time comes for me to move on. It's a continuation of Alateen with the same kind of warm and understanding people. I want to keep growing for the rest of my life and Al-Anon can help me do just that.

Sometimes I take offense at everything my parents say to me. They tell me I'm too sensitive, but ugly words and shouting matches have a way of really hurting me.

The program is helping me to see that when they explode, it's part of the illness that has our home life in chaos. When I react, it only makes things worse.

I've found a good way to accept things I can't handle and I'm trying to put it into practice now. I think of my reactions as a light switch. When things are going well, I leave it "on" and let myself get involved and have a good time. But when they're not, I can turn the switch "off" so my parents' anger doesn't get inside me. That makes it easier to listen to what they're saying so we can sit down and discuss it later.

Things to Think About

Just because my parents are angry, it doesn't mean I have to be. When I stop reacting to what they're saying, their words can't hurt me as much. Today I'll try to understand why my parents get angry and keep loving them in spite of it.

Growing in the program is like living our early years all over again. First we learn to walk. With each Step we take, we grow a little stronger until we're able to walk straight and tall.

Then we learn to talk. Instead of shouting and screaming, we learn to communicate from the heart, a little at a time, until we can share how we feel inside.

Finally, we learn to go out into the world and stand on our own feet. We start to think for ourselves and be responsible for our own actions. It's not always easy. Sometimes we fall and scrape our knees. But that doesn't keep us down for long, because we know the only way to keep growing is to get up and move ahead!

Things to Think About

Now that I'm in Alateen I'm starting to grow on the inside. It takes time. The Twelve Steps give me a sense of direction and help to keep me growing, one step at a time.

I was really bitter during my first few weeks in Alateen. My questions were endless: "Why do I have to watch my father drink himself to death? Why do I have to listen to all the senseless arguments when most of my friends are enjoying a good night's sleep? Why do I have to put up with being shoved around and yelled at all the time?" By others sharing with me, I realized the alcoholic was suffering from a disease that affected our whole family, but even that didn't seem to help *me* very much. I was just sick and tired of hurting so much and I wanted to run away from it all.

I'm glad I didn't. I stayed around and found myself a personal Sponsor. We spent a lot of time talking about the hurt I was carrying inside. With his help, I started to understand that while there wasn't much I could do to change the situation at home, I could change my reaction to it. I could protect myself from being hurt by trying to detach, refusing to let things get to my insides.

Things to Think About

If I wanted to feel better, I have to find a way to get rid of my hurts instead of letting them rattle around inside me. A good Sponsor can help. When we work the program together, I learn how to rise above the pain and understand what's happening to me and the rest of my family.

When I came to Alateen, someone told me we all needed to believe in a Power greater than ourselves. I didn't buy it. For a long time I'd been used to getting along just fine on my own and I didn't need anyone to look after me.

It took time before I started to change my attitude. When things were bad I relied on the people in my group. That's where I found the strength I needed.

Now I find I need a personal Power—Someone I can talk to each day. I realize it's a silent conversation on His part, but something about it works for me. Good things are happening in my life and I know it has a lot to do with a special kind of personal contact I have with my Higher Power.

Things to Think About

No one tells me what to believe in Alateen. That's a good feeling, especially if I'm having trouble believing in anything. When I need something, there are plenty of places to turn. I can start by believing in the program and the people in my group. In time, I might find a personal Power greater than myself to help me through each day.

We come to Alateen with a big problem we can't handle by ourselves. That's okay because in Alateen we pull together to help each other.

For many of us, it's the first time in a long while that we've let ourselves trust other people. We've been used to feeling cut off from everybody, unneeded, unwanted, and afraid to count on anybody or anything. Now we're part of something where togetherness counts. We're needed and trusted. We belong to a group of people helping people.

Each of us gets some of our strength from the group, so the stronger the group is, the more strength we can get. This is one of the reasons why what's good for the group has to come first—even before the good of any one person.

Things to Think About

All of us deserve the opportunity to grow. One of the ways we get this chance is by working together to make our group strong. Tradition One calls it unity; it's really pulling together to help each other and remembering that *we* and *our* are a lot stronger than *me* and *my*.

When alcoholism ran wild in my home, I spent so much time thinking about the alcoholic that I never took time to think about myself. I kept waiting for everybody else to look after me and when they didn't, I resented them for ignoring me. I really let myself go downhill. I sat in front of the television for so long that my mind was like a sponge. I didn't get enough rest, I ate a lot of junk, and my appearance was a disaster. No wonder people wanted to have little or nothing to do with me!

Now I know there are things I need to do to keep myself alive and healthy. I'm responsible for my own mind and body. I *can* take care of myself and I can do it without blaming others for not doing the job for me. I can keep my mind alert, get the proper rest, and eat the right food. Keeping my insides and outsides in good shape is one way I can show that I really care about me.

Things to Think About

When my mind is so tied up with another person that I don't care about myself, I'm off the track and need to make some changes. When I take the time to look after me first, I'm well on my way to finding something I've always wanted: self-respect.

The world is like a box crammed with the hustle and bustle of living. For a long time I believed there was no escape from this "boxed-in" feeling. Then I realized that I could make things happier for myself in the box, if I really tried.

I started to watch other people. Some got their happiness from religion, but I wasn't ready for that. Others tried to get it by taking drugs, but when they came out of their dreamworld they found themselves in the same spot or worse. Others tried to buy their happiness by using money and power, but that didn't seem to work either.

Then I came to Alateen. I found friends there who really cared about me. I thought I'd found the secret to being happy. But the happiness didn't last long. I couldn't understand why until I heard someone say, "You only get out of it what you put into it." Now I realize that I have to work for what I want; things aren't going to come to me on a silver platter.

Things to Think About

If I'm looking for the secret to happiness, I can stop today. It's no secret—I have to make my own happiness. Working the program will help me do just that.

My parents had a lot of trouble facing the problem in our home. None of us ever really dealt with our feelings; we just tried to make everything look good. I played the game, too. I seemed fine on the outside. In fact, I was an overachiever. But deep inside I kept my anger and fear hidden. One day I snapped; years of pent-up feelings flooded out and I cried for hours. I ended up in the hospital under the care of a psychiatrist.

There was an Al-Anon meeting at the hospital and the doctor made sure I got to it. The people there listened and understood how I felt. They told me about Alateen and made arrangements for some members to take me to a meeting when I was released.

It feels good now to be able to say how I feel. I still slip back into my old way of thinking, but at least I can talk about it and I'm learning to laugh at myself, too.

Things to Think About

It's hard to act as if everything is okay when it's not. When I keep stuffing my feelings down inside, something has to give and it's usually me. In Alateen I don't have to hide anymore. I can talk about my feelings and learn to handle them in a way that's good for me.

I didn't believe my problems could be solved. Sometimes, when I'm feeling lazy or confused, I still think that way.

Now I know there are solutions to my problems, but it's up to me to do something about finding them. I try to tackle my problems "One Day at a Time" with the help of my Higher Power and my Alateen friends. Talking about the slogans and the Steps at meetings helps a lot, too. I'm like a child learning to walk. Each time I fall, I need the courage to pick myself up and keep going, knowing that the next fall won't hurt as much.

I'm learning that things do get better according to how much effort I put into improving myself. As I try to do that a little more each day, I'm starting to find a bit of serenity and many of my problems are taking care of themselves.

Things to Think About

Alateen gives me a way to solve my problems, but I have to choose how hard I want to work at it. It's not easy; it takes courage and patience. But if I try hard today I'll get over the rough spots and start to realize how much Alateen can do for me if I let it.

After years of living with an alcoholic, I'd given up hope for myself and my family. I'd tried everything—tears, screams, threats, and leaving home. I'd even tried to kill myself, but nothing seemed to work.

Then I read about Alateen in our school newspaper. The article talked about a fellowship for teenagers living with an alcoholic. I was desperate enough to try anything, so I went.

I found the hope I'd lost. People understood me and accepted me as I was. They gave me love and kept on giving it even when I rejected it. Most of all, they showed me how to change myself by using the program. This was the key to my learning how to live and it still is today.

Things to Think About

Without the program I wouldn't have made it this far. It's given me the chance to "live again." Because of what it's done for me, I want to share it with other people who feel as desperate as I once did. Doing that is my way of saying "thank you" to Alateen.

By the time I'd been in Alateen a month, I was glowing from the effects of the program. My new friends gave me comfort and relief by sharing the Steps, the Serenity Prayer, and the slogans, but it was mainly their warm understanding that kept me coming back. They accepted me and showed me love and I learned to trust them.

When I started attending conventions, district meetings, and assemblies, I met a lot of Al-Anon people whose stories attracted me in many ways. They reminded me of my parents and talked of having the same problems, needs, and hopes as me. They shared their experience, strength, and hope. They helped me see that the Steps are the principles that bind us together, regardless of our age. And their honesty reached something deep inside where I had seldom been touched before. I realized then that there was a place for me in Al-Anon.

Things to Think About

Sometimes it's hard to think about moving from Alateen to Al-Anon. I enjoy being with my Alateen friends and I want to postpone growing up. It helps to remember that we're all part of Al-Anon. When I'm ready to move on, I won't be leaving my Alateen friends behind; I'll just be getting to know another group of friends who can help me grow up and get what I need out of the program.

When I first came to Alateen I used to get upset when someone would say, "That's *their* problem." *Their* problem was bothering me, too!

After awhile, it dawned on me that my friends were really talking about the last line of the Serenity Prayer. Realizing "whose problem is whose" is having the wisdom to know the difference between what I can change and what I have to accept. Other people's problems are mine only when I don't know, or don't want to know, the difference.

I need courage to change *my* attitude and behavior. The Serenity Prayer can help me. And, if I make it a part of my thinking every day, it will remind me that I can't fix *their* problems; that's up to *them*.

Things to Think About

I can only change one life—my own. The Serenity Prayer makes that clear. It helps me to accept the things I can't change and gives me the courage to change my thinking and actions. Best of all it gives me the wisdom that helps me to mind my own business today.

After my father joined A.A., I thought he was great. But I hated my mother. She just had to glance at me when she was shouting and I'd immediately think she was blaming me for everything. She used to make a lot of excuses about why my father came home late, but as soon as he'd walk in, she'd scream at him. I felt sorry for him and thought, "No wonder he drank so much with her on his back." One day I asked him why he didn't divorce her so he and I could live on our own. That's when he suggested I try Alateen.

The program helped me realize that the problems in our home caused by alcoholism affected our whole family. When I started to understand just how deeply my mother had been affected, I stopped hating her. I realized I had forgiven my father for everything he'd done, but I hadn't thought to do that with my mother. Today I get along better with my mother. She's taking an interest in me as a person and I'm trying to do the same with her.

Things to Think About

Learning about the *family illness* shows me that we're *all* affected. When I accept that, it will be the start of rebuilding my relationship with the nonalcoholic and the rest of my family.

It's about eighteen inches from my brain to my heart, but sometimes that's the longest eighteen inches I've ever known. When I hear an idea in the program, I think about it and turn it over in my mind a few times. After awhile, I start to understand it, but it's not until I accept it that it becomes a part of my everyday life.

It was that way for me with learning to detach by using the First Step. I'd hear a lot about it at meetings and understood what it meant. I could even *admit* that I was powerless over alcohol and that I had an unmanageable life. But admitting was as far as it went. It wasn't until later, after practicing the Steps several times, that I started to *accept* the fact that I was powerless. That was the key that helped me detach, in my heart as well as my brain, and really let go.

Things to Think About
The heart is where I live. It's easy to be a thinker in the program. Sometimes I can even impress people with my fantastic brain. But when I feel the program *from the heart,* I can accept it as my way of life.

"Easy Does It" is a great slogan to use every day. It helps to calm us down when we're frustrated. We can use it at home with our family, in our work at school, and even in our daily chores.

One member shared with his Alateen group how he used the slogan when he washes the dishes. "It's Sunday evening and my turn to do the dishes. With eight people in our family, no automatic dishwasher, and dishes from breakfast, lunch, and dinner, it's a big job! The piles of dishes seem endless and I start to feel smothered by the task.

"Then I remember "Easy Does It" and a calm comes over me. I separate everything and wash the cups first, then the bowls, then the plates, the silverware, and the pots—one thing at a time. Before I know it the job's done!"

Things to Think About

When there's a big job ahead of me, it's easy to become discouraged before I start. When I take things one at a time, in little bits, the job doesn't seem so overwhelming after all and I'm finished in no time. The secret to getting things done: "Easy Does It."

I used to react every time someone tried to pick a fight with me. I'd start fighting back with my fists and my mouth, but I'd only end up getting confused and making a fool of myself.

Now I'm learning to walk away instead. Turning my will and life over to the care of my Higher Power helps me a lot. Every morning I use Step Three and make a decision to "Let Go and Let God." How much I'm willing to let go determines how relaxed my day is. If I give my Higher Power 50%, He's only got half of me to work with and I can't expect terrific results. But if I let Him have all of me—100%—I believe He'll guide me in everything I do for the rest of the day, especially the tense times when I'm tempted to start reacting again.

Things to Think About

Alone, I can't stop myself from reacting when people are on my back about something. But I can do it with the help of my Higher Power. When I'm willing to let go all the way and let God give me a helping hand, I can get rid of my short fuse and calm down.

I hear again and again at meetings that alcoholism is a disease. I may even say it to others, but sometimes I still think that the alcoholic in my family is my enemy.

I need Alateen to remind me that an attitude like that really hurts me and can never do anything to improve our family situation. Instead, I have to remember that the alcoholic is sick. It's unfair of me to judge him and try to get back at him because we don't punish people for being sick.

I have to let go of the alcoholic and start working on myself. It isn't easy because there are still times when I feel "he's out to get me" and I want to strike back. But with the help of Step One and the Serenity Prayer, I'm starting to *accept* what I hear at meetings about "detaching with love" and I'm trying to put it into practice in my life.

Things to Think About

I have to use a "hands-off policy" with the alcoholic and concentrate on improving myself. It's hard to do, but it works when I listen to others talk about their experiences with detachment and try to apply their ideas to my own situation. I can cope with my problems today by changing my thinking about the alcoholic and by letting him take care of his own problems while I look after mine.

When I took the Fourth Step, it wasn't easy to admit I had any faults. I wanted to forget about some of them. I didn't even want to admit them to myself. But I had to be honest.

I took my inventory and found a lot of shortcomings. But there was a lot of good there, too. That gave me a boost and it was easier to face my faults.

Once I admitted my defects to myself, I started to see how I could improve myself. I put them in a list and started to work on them, one at a time, a little each day.

Things to Think About

I have got a lot of faults, but there's a lot of good inside me, too. Taking an honest inventory shows me both sides. When I see the positive things about me, it's easier to face the negative and do something about improving myself today.

I used to bounce up and down from one extreme to another. If everything was going fine, I'd think I was perfect. I could do no wrong; I was the best at everything, and had answers for everyone. But if things turned sour, I'd think there was something wrong with me. I could do nothing right and I didn't have answers for anyone.

By the time I came to the fellowship, I was exhausted from acting like a yo-yo. Through the program I started to find a happy medium in my life. I learned to accept myself—good and bad alike—and realized that what happens outside of me doesn't have to determine what kind of person I am.

I have good and bad days. I'm terrific at doing some things and terrible at others. I have answers for some people, but only questions for most. Through all of this I know I'm neither perfect nor rotten. I'm somewhere in between and that feels a lot more comfortable than before.

Things to Think About

Many of the ups and downs in my life are natural. Instead of letting them drag me up and down with them, I'll try to get my feet on solid ground. Finding a happy medium between the extremes will help me remember that I'm a good person regardless of what's going on around me.

It's not easy to forgive, especially if I have some big resentments. But if I accept alcoholism as an illness, I know that people do certain things because they're sick. Understanding this can be the beginning of getting rid of some of my resentments.

I want to be forgiven for my mistakes, so I need to learn to forgive others, too. It can be a part of my Seventh Step. While I'm asking my Higher Power to forgive me, I can ask Him to help me forgive.

Forgiving the alcoholic and other people isn't something I do with words alone. It comes from the heart. When it does, I can let go of my resentments and get on with improving my relationships.

Things to Think About

I don't want other people to hold grudges against me, so it's up to me to let go of my bad feelings about them. Step Seven is a good place to start. Asking God to forgive me for the mistakes I've made helps me to forgive others for what they've done to me. Forgiving other people helps me to deal with my resentments.

I get a lot out of going to meetings. If I have a problem at school, I know I can go to my parents for advice, but they finished school long ago and they can't really identify with me.

My Alateen friends can. Usually they help me see how using the program can solve the problem. But even if no one really knows what to do, I still feel better just talking about it. That helps me to have a lot more confidence at school. When we have discussions, I can take part willingly now instead of sitting back and listening to everyone else.

Things to Think About

Talking things over with my Alateen friends has helped me to speak up at school. When I have a problem, I go to the people who understand—Alateens—knowing they'll guide me to the parts of the program that can help me solve my problem.

The Ninth Step is the action that follows the plans we made to make amends in Step Eight. We start moving and try to apologize for the mistakes we've made in our relationships with people. When the past is brought up we say we're sorry and then try to show in our *actions* that we really have changed.

It's not always possible to make amends. People may have died or moved away; sometimes we'd only be hurting other people to make ourselves feel better. In these cases we do what we can and then start living today with a special love for the people who are important to us. They'll see by our *actions* that we care.

Things to Think About

Step Nine helps me to say I'm sorry to those I've hurt. I can face up to my mistakes, put them behind me, and try to live a new life following the program.

Before Alateen I had a bad attitude about a lot of things. I didn't care about what I said or did to other people, especially my family and friends. Sometimes I treated them like dirt.

Now I realize that other people treat me the same way I treat them. If I want things to be different, it's up to me to change my attitude. I'll be a lot happier with myself if I do, and it will be easier for other people to get along with me.

Things to Think About

Instead of trying to criticize other people, I'll concentrate on improving my own life today. I'll try not to hurt people by what I say and do. Sometimes I might have to bite my tongue, but things will go a lot better if I remember to mind my own business and "Live and Let Live."

When I'm walking to school in the morning, I have a lot of time to think. I try to plan my day, all the good things I can do, and all the bad things I don't want to do.

It's a good opportunity for me to practice the Eleventh Step. I try to "plug in" to my Higher Power. I think about the good things He's given me. I remember what I was like when I came to Alateen and thank Him that I'm not like that anymore. Then I try to keep quiet and listen to what He's saying to me.

Talking and listening to my Higher Power on the way to school gives me a real lift. It gets me moving in the right direction and I walk through the doors in a great frame of mind, ready to start the day.

Things to Think About

Getting in touch with my Higher Power can happen anywhere and anytime. When I try to make contact in the morning, it gets me ready for the whole day. Saying thanks and asking for His help reminds me that He's the strength behind everything I do today.

When my father came home from his Al-Anon meeting one night, he put some pamphlets on the kitchen table. Being curious, I wondered what they were, so I took a look at them.

It was Alateen literature. Right away, it intrigued me. It gave me the message that I wasn't alone— other people had been through the same things I had. Somewhere I read the words "we understand" and I made up my mind to go and find out just how true that really was.

So I went to my first Alateen meeting the next week. At first the people were unfamiliar and I was a little uncomfortable. But when they started opening up and sharing with me, I got to know each one of them and now we're great friends. I know now that what I read is absolutely true—they really do understand.

Things to Think About

Literature is the "voice of the fellowship" in print. It carries the message of hope and understanding. When I go to meetings, I hear that same message again and again. It's put into action by people, like me, who really care.

I played a lot of golf this summer. Sometimes I did well, but most of the time I was frustrated because I didn't play consistently. Eventually I realized I wouldn't play any better until I practiced my golf every day to get the skills I needed.

That's a lot like the last part of Step Twelve. Practicing the principles of the program in *all* my affairs can make a big difference in my life. If I'm willing to try, a lot of the daily ups and downs will be replaced by a steady desire to grow.

Things to Think About

Daily practice is important in anything I want to do well. Why should it be any different with my program? If I make it part of everything I do, I'll start to even out the highs and lows in my life.

Newcomers to Alateen usually feel alone in a hostile world, drowning in a sea of troubles. They don't realize that they've caused many of their own problems. All of us have to learn about the disease of alcoholism before we can start to feel calm and peaceful inside of ourselves. It takes time.

Newcomers are special people. When they come to Alateen, they enrich our lives as well as their own. But let's not be too quick to swamp these confused people with a lot of advice. A warm welcome and words of hope will be all they can use at first. That will keep them coming back. Deeper thoughts can come later when the time is right.

Things to Think About

When I was a newcomer, it was feelings more than words that made me want to come back to Alateen. The love and acceptance told me I belonged here. Today I'll take time to welcome somebody new to the fellowship. It will help both of us to remember that we belong to a group of very special people.

Sometimes we're so concerned about the unity in our group that we forget what Tradition One really means. We gang up on people who have a different opinion than the rest of the group and try to force them to change their minds or we simply ignore their ideas.

Unity doesn't mean everyone has to think the same way. One of the great things about Alateen is that all of us have the right to say what we think and feel. That's part of what makes our group strong and united.

When people have different opinions, we don't have to argue with them. We need to listen to them and think carefully about what they're saying. Then, when all of us have had a chance to share our ideas, we vote as we wish and go with the majority decision. That's what guides the group. Those who feel differently have said so and we all start to work together to keep the ground united.

Things to Think About

I want other people to respect my opinion and I have to respect theirs. If we understand our differences, it can be a real strength. In Alateen we call that unity, and it comes from understanding and practicing Tradition One.

Leaving home? Not a very easy decision to make, is it? Decisions that affect the rest of our lives aren't easy. Sometimes we have to make difficult choices like where to live, whom to live with, what to be, and where to work.

We need self-confidence and a strong will. The program can help. We can rely on our Higher Power and our Alateen group. Sharing a problem makes it only half a problem.

No one ever said growing up was going to be smooth sailing, but it's a lot easier with a Higher Power and our Alateen friends to help us.

Things to Think About

Life is full of choices, especially when I'm just ready to move out into the world. It's not easy to make decisions by myself. The program gives me a Higher Power and a great group of friends. Today I'll ask for their help.

I used to make excuses for everything: Not having my homework done, not returning money I had borrowed, not coming home on time. Making excuses was my way of getting out of trouble, but when I made them, I felt guilty. It stayed on my conscience for a long time because it was just like telling a lie.

Now I'm learning to be honest. Instead of trying to make excuses for myself, I'm trying to tell it like it is. I've stopped playing games and I feel a lot better now because I'm not hiding behind my excuses.

Things to Think About

Making excuses is selfish. When I do it, I'm only trying to cover myself. Alateen tells me to be honest—to be responsible for my actions. It takes less energy to tell the truth and it works out better for everybody concerned.

Before Alateen I was afraid to live. I probably wouldn't have committed suicide, but I built a wall around myself to keep from getting hurt and rarely went outside of it. I just existed from one day to the next. I lived that way because it was safe.

Alateen loved me back to life. It gave me the courage to stick my neck out from behind my wall and take risks. I found that life wasn't as scary as I thought.

The Twelve Steps have given my life a real purpose and the Serenity Prayer has given me a deep love for my Higher Power who guides my life. I realize now that life is for living and I try to do a lot of it each day.

Things to Think About

When I live a sheltered life, I miss the whole point of living. Alateen helps me to break out of my shell and find out what life is really all about. There's a lot to it and with the help of the program, I'll have the courage to live it every day.

I'm a great procrastinator! I love to put things off as long as I can. Sometimes, leaving things until it's too late gets me into trouble: an assignment at school, an important job around the house, a call to a special friend.

When my mind is still working on yesterday's responsibilities, I can't concentrate on today. Alateen is a *today* program. If I want to get the most out of it, I have to stop stalling and get moving. Reading the Alateen *Just For Today* pamphlet is a good place to start. Its message is as simple as the old saying "Don't put off till tomorrow what you can do today."

Things to Think About

If I have a letter to write, a book to read, homework to finish, or some cleaning up to do, I'll do it *now* instead of waiting till later. Trying to live "Just for Today" will take away a lot of worry and frustration and make today a better day.

Why do I have to go to Alateen? Why can't someone else's parent be an alcoholic instead of mine?

At times I still feel angry and sorry for myself because my parent has a drinking problem. I think everybody has an easier life than me. Then I remember that having an alcoholic parent brought me to Alateen in the first place. It gave me a chance to find a way of life that can help me through my teenage years and that's something I can be grateful for.

Things to Think About

Instead of complaining because I live with an alcoholic, I'll try to accept that fact and think of it as an opportunity to make something of my life. Not every teenager has the chance to use such a program to work out everyday problems. I'm thankful that I'm one of the lucky ones.

If I want help from my Higher Power, I have to be willing to put forth some effort. I believe He'll provide me with the tools, but I have to keep watching for opportunities to use them.

When I have a problem, I look to my Higher Power. I pray, then I sit and wait. But most times the answer just doesn't come; I have to take some action. I can go to a meeting and start talking about what's on my mind. Or, I can sit down with my Sponsor and discuss how to handle what's bothering me. Before I know it, I've found some workable answers for the problem and I'm on my way to solving it.

Things to Think About

I just can't pray and expect to get answers immediately. But I can look for them among the members of my Alateen group, in the literature I read, and in a lot of other places. The key is to start looking. Not all the answers I hear will be right for me, but if I keep searching, I'll probably find the ones I need to solve any problem I'm facing.

How can I give the gift of love to others if I don't love myself? Acceptance is the key. When I accept myself for who I am, I can start to love myself again. It's a special kind of freedom that grows when I'm willing to take an honest look at myself and change for the better.

Loving myself makes it possible to love other people. I can accept them and let them learn from their own mistakes. That doesn't mean I can't talk with or help them, but I have to be able to let them decide what's best for themselves. That way they have their freedom and I still have mine, and the love between us can grow.

Real love happens when people feel free to be themselves. It's a beautiful thing that starts with acceptance and grows as I work the program for myself and live it in my relationships with other people.

Things to Think About

When I give myself the freedom to be me, I can give it away to others. This is called acceptance and it's the key to love in the program. It opens the door to loving myself and lets me share that love with the people around me.

My father died drunk. I hadn't seen him for a long time, but it still hurt when I heard the news. At first I felt sorry for him for all he'd been through. Then I hated him because he'd left us alone. Then I remembered the First Step and tried to stay calm instead of getting wound up tight. It wasn't easy letting go, but as I thought about the Step, I realized I could accept the fact that some alcoholics die without ever finding sobriety.

Now that my father is dead, do I still need the program? You bet I do, more than ever! *My* life isn't over. In fact, it's really just begun and I know I'm going to need the program every day to keep my life moving in a positive direction.

Things to Think About

Even if I'm no longer living with an alcoholic, I still belong here because Alateen is a program for me. It's my way of life. Without it, I'd be struggling to "pick up the pieces." But with the help of the Steps and the rest of the program, I can handle even the most painful situations and go on living each day.

I always looked for bad qualities in people. I judged them by their appearance and, as a result, I never had any friends. When new people came to our class at school, I would take one look at them and see all the bad. Immediately I would decide not to associate with them. That was before I came to Alateen.

Now, with the help of the program, I'm learning to be a lot more tolerant of others. Personality means more to me than a person's appearance; it's their insides that count. I try to look for people's good points instead of singling out their bad ones. Today I'm finding that many of the people I avoided are really kind of nice. In fact some of them are now good friends of mine.

Things to Think About

The old saying, "Don't judge a book by its cover" is a good one for me. I want to be accepted as I am, so I have to be willing to do the same for others. That means looking past the outside and getting to know a person on the inside. As I become less critical of others by working the program today, I'll find it easier to make friends and people will be a lot more friendly toward me.

When I first came to Alateen, I didn't believe in a Higher Power. I couldn't understand how anybody could be so cruel as to put me in the kind of life I was living. Because I was full of fear and didn't trust anyone, I was locked up in my own little world, completely shut off from everyone.

In Step Two I realized that there was help for me. I kept an open mind and began to understand that no one was to blame for my situation at home. Gradually, I started to believe in a Power greater than myself and bit by bit He brought a little balance into my life.

My Higher Power really does exist and His help is there for me whenever I need it. The care and understanding in the program is also a great help. I'm still working on being restored to sanity. To me it simply means getting happy with myself.

Things to Think About

I used to think my Higher Power wanted the worst for me. Now I believe He wants to help me. That help is mine today if I ask for it. I'll find it in Step Two and in the love of my Alateen friends.

I'm really trying to change myself, but sometimes I try to do too much at once. I end up feeling sorry for myself and have a hard time getting out of that mood.

I need to take things "One Day at a Time" and remember that this day belongs to me. Nobody in the world has one just like it. How I handle it is up to me. I can ruin it with negative thoughts or I can put in some happy thoughts to make it a good day.

If my problems seem too big for me to handle, I'll ask my Higher Power to help me with them. I don't even have to explain everything. He can tell what's on my mind and He knows what's best for me.

Things to Think About

When I get too far ahead of myself, I feel frustrated and self-pity takes over. My problems turn into mountains and I feel weighed down. How I handle them makes a big difference. When I try to live "One Day at a Time" and ask my Higher Power for help, the load is a lot lighter. I feel better about myself and I can make today into something really special.

I want to be good to myself, but it's easier said than done. Sometimes it's hard to stop reliving the rotten times in my life. And it's not always easy to stop resenting and blaming others for everything that happens to me.

No one asks me to carry such a big load of bad feelings. So why do I? Dwelling on my troubles only makes me hurt more.

Maybe I need to give myself a special treat: a good laugh. I may not feel much like laughing, but if I try to find even a little humor in my problems, it can have a surprising effect on my attitude. It *can* make the hurt go away and help me get to the bottom of the problem a lot faster.

Things to Think About
When I have a problem, nothing seems very funny. But sometimes my biggest problem is that I take myself too seriously. A bit of humor might be just the thing I need to find my way through my troubles. It can lift my spirits and give me a new look at something that's been weighing me down for a long time.

Sometimes I still hate the alcoholic. Because she's still drinking, I can't do anything. I have to look after my brothers and sisters at home so I can't get involved in anything at school. I don't have any friends and the teachers are always on my back because I don't get my homework done. Some days I just want to pack it all in and take off. All I really want is a little time for myself.

Then I remember my Alateen group. It's like a home away from home to me; my friends there understand. They keep in touch with me when I can't get out of the house. They accept me and want to help me. Their caring makes me want to dig deeper into the program and start working the Steps. When I do, some of the hate goes away. I take a little time for me, call my Sponsor, and work on changing my attitude.

Things to Think About

When I feel weighed down by all my responsibilities at home, it's easy to be resentful. But what does it get me? I'm the one that's miserable when I feel this way. Staying in touch with my friends in the fellowship can make the load seem a bit lighter. As a result, a lot of the energy I was putting into my resentments can be used to make me happy.

OCT **OCTOBER 3** [277

Sometimes I think other people are better off than I am. They have things I don't have; they get all the good breaks.

When I concentrate on what I don't have, I feel inferior. I start to run myself down and I feel jealous of other people.

Alateen shows me I have a lot to be grateful for. When I look at the "good" column in my inventory and thank my Higher Power for all the gifts I've been given, it's hard to be jealous. There will always be people who have better *things* than I do, but nobody can take away the good that's inside of me.

Things to Think About

I can't be jealous and grateful at the same time. Instead of comparing myself to other people today, I'll be thankful for all that Alateen has given me and realize that I'm a good person. The more I respect myself, the easier it will be to accept good things in the lives of other people.

When we were little and trying to walk, it all started with our first step. In Alateen we have Steps to take, too. But before we can get to the rest of the Steps, we have to take the First. It's just as important as when we started walking because it shows that we're trying to change the way we think. Our lives are a mess because we've been trying so hard to fix the alcoholic's problems that we haven't had time for our own. Now we admit that we're powerless; we can't do anything to change the alcoholic or anyone else, but we *can* start to do something about ourselves.

Sometimes it's hard to take the First Step. If we trip, it doesn't hurt to get back up, dust ourselves off, and start all over again. When we begin to accept alcoholism as a disease and admit that *our* lives need changing, a new world opens up to us—the world of Alateen. It's our first step on the road to a better way of life.

Things to Think About

The program won't mean as much to me until I take the First Step. When I stop concentrating on the alcoholic's problems and start doing something about my own life, it opens the door to a new way of life for me.

It's good to set high standards for myself, but I have to be realistic about it. I get frustrated when I expect too much of myself. I think I'm some kind of superperson who can solve all life's problems overnight.

When I feel that way about myself, I start expecting too much of other people, too. I have great plans for them and when they don't measure up, I feel let down and angry.

Alateen shows me how to aim high and remember "Easy Does It" at the same time. I'm starting to take a good look at what I've got planned for myself. The program is helping me to relax and be a bit more realistic about what I expect of myself and other people.

Things to Think About

Sometimes I have to settle for less than I'd like and be willing to accept it. I won't expect too much of anyone today, not even myself. I'll take it easy and set my goals just a little lower so I can enjoy doing the things I do.

The first time I took my inventory, I only did it on the surface and forgot about everything else. I was as honest as I could be at the time, but skimming the surface was only the beginning. In time I learned to dig a little deeper. It was like going into the water knee-deep instead of sticking my toes in around the edges. Growing in the program gave me the courage to look at who I really was.

Now I find that whenever something is bothering me—if I'm getting into a fight—I stop and ask myself, "What am *I* doing to cause this fight? What's making me feel and act this way?" I just take what I need at the time instead of drawing it out and doing my whole inventory at once. Doing things this way, I find my character defects are easier to face and I'm a lot more honest with myself.

Things to Think About

Taking an inventory is more than "scratching the surface." It calls for taking a deeper look at myself. I need a lot of courage to do that. I can sit down and do it all at once, but sometimes it's easier if I take it in little bits. No matter how I do it, trying to be honest is the key. It will help me face the truth about myself and accept responsibility for my actions.

"It's the alcoholic's problem—not mine!" How many times have we heard a newcomer say just that? Maybe we've said it ourselves. But after feeling trapped in a battle between our parents and watching the love in our family turn to hatred, we know that the problem is *ours*, not just the alcoholic's.

When we learn in Alateen that alcoholism is a family illness, it makes a lot of sense. What a relief to know there's a reason for the way we feel about things!

Our whole family has been affected by alcoholism. Now with the program, we can help by concentrating on our own recovery.

Things to Think About

I'm part of a family that's been affected by alcoholism. The best thing I can do for myself is to work the program each day. As I "get better," my change of attitude *just might* help others in my family, including the alcoholic.

Alateens are special people because they—

*A*lways help me with my problems,
*L*isten when I need to talk,
*A*ccept me as I am,
*T*ry to help me understand alcoholism,
*E*ncourage me with their caring,
*E*njoy being with me,
*N*otice me and remind me that I'm special, too!

Things to Think About

The love and friendship in Alateen can't be found in any ordinary group of teenagers. I feel accepted, needed, and important to other people. Alateens have helped me to turn my life around because they care.

Sometimes my parents seem so old-fashioned in their thinking. I'm growing up, but they still treat me like a child. I wish they'd wake up and realize we're living in the twenty-first century.

At one time feelings like that made it hard for me to love my parents, but the program is helping me to see it's a natural part of growing up. I'm learning to respect the differences between us. I don't always agree with what they think, but deep inside I know they want the best for me and I want the best for them.

One good sign: There's no more "I'll love you *if*" or, "I'll love you *when*" in our conversations. I think we're learning to love each other in spite of our differences and that's helping to make all of us better people.

Things to Think About

I can't expect my parents or anyone else to be what I want them to be. They're human beings and they deserve my respect. I don't have to like all their actions, but I can love them for who they are and let that be the key to our relationship.

Honesty is something I need to practice. Without it, I wouldn't be able to trust anyone.

It took me a long time to surrender and be honest with myself, but once I did, I started getting a lot more out of Alateen. I accepted myself as I really was. I trusted myself to do things and I had a lot more faith in myself as a person.

Being honest with myself helps me to be more honest with other people, too. They trust me and I trust them. We open up to each other, share our deep feelings, and start to build some solid friendships in Alateen.

Things to Think About

Little white lies have a way of building up until they cloud the real truth. Being honest cuts through all that. Alateen shows me how to be honest. The more honest I am today, the easier it will be to trust myself and others as I grow in the program.

Sometimes things get out of hand at our meetings. Some people want to fool around and turn the meeting into a social hour. Then, when the meeting finally gets going, a few people do all the talking and never give others a chance to share. I feel the resentment building up inside me and I want to say something. Then I remember that Tradition One says it better than I can: "Our common welfare should come first; personal progress for the greatest number depends upon unity."

I know I'm not the only one who came here looking for help, but my life depends on what I get out of the program and the meetings are a big part of that. When a few people get out of line, it hurts everyone.

The group is only as strong as its weakest link. That's why we need to listen to the First Tradition. If we work together, the way the Tradition says, we can make ours the kind of group where all of us can get the help we need.

Things to Think About

Tradition One tells the story of every meeting: We need to stick together to help each other. If I take this Tradition seriously, I'll be doing my part to keep the group together.

When trouble comes my way it's easy to let my old feelings of fear and worry get hold of me. I let myself get tired and worn out. I can't even think straight.

That's when I need to remember "Let Go and Let God." If I've done all I can in a situation, I can leave the results up to God and trust Him to carry me through the day. He did it yesterday and the day before—so why not today?

Things may not turn out my way, but it's good to know that they'll turn out the way they're supposed to.

Things to Think About

When I've done my best to solve a problem and things aren't getting any better, I know it's time to say, "Hey, God, this one is up to You!" If I do the groundwork, He'll take care of the end results.

When a member asks me to be his personal Sponsor, the message is loud and clear. It's as if he's saying, "I trust you!" For a long time, I couldn't even trust myself, let alone have other people trust me. So being someone's Sponsor means a lot to me.

As a Sponsor I'm learning to listen without giving advice. I can try to understand what the other person is going through and respond to what he's feeling without getting all tangled up in his troubles. I can share his pain and fear and I tell him how the program has helped me deal with similar situations.

Sponsorship is a special kind of relationship with a lot of rewards. The best one of all is watching another person grow as he starts to use the Alateen ideas in his life each day.

Things to Think About

Sponsoring somebody is more than just being good friends with him. It's an opportunity to help that person make sense of his life; it's a relationship built on trust. If I'm willing to accept that trust and share my growth in the program with another person, a lot of special rewards can be mine.

I couldn't find any good points when I took my first inventory. That was pretty scary, so I just covered up my faults and left them alone.

Through Alateen I learned that when I found a fault in myself, I had to admit it was a problem and work on it right away. I started to face things as they came up instead of putting them off and that became my way of doing the Tenth Step. I stopped thinking that I was all bad because I was only looking at one thing at a time instead of a lot of things as once.

It took awhile, but I finally found a few positive qualities about myself. That boosted my self-confidence and gave me the strength to keep working on myself each day.

Things to Think About

When something negative comes up, Step Ten helps me take care of it right away, instead of putting if off and getting stuck with a lot of bad thoughts later. I feel a lot happier since I've learned to apply the Tenth Step in my life every day.

I was the kind of person who couldn't tell others that I was angry. I kept everything locked inside and stewed and boiled for days. Sometimes the pressure would be so bad that I'd actually feel as if I was going to explode. Then some little thing would happen and I'd blow up at the nearest person and cause a lot of hard feelings.

In Alateen I'm learning a way to prevent that. Instead of putting things off, I try to go to the people involved in the situation and talk about my angry feelings. Sometimes I yell, but most of the time I can discuss things without too much fuss. I'm able to get things out in the open. It must be working because my insides don't ache the way they used to.

Things to Think About

When I'm used to keeping the lid on my feelings, it's not easy to start talking about them, but it's a big help if I can. Instead of keeping anger and resentment locked inside, I can get them out, talk them over with someone else, and start handling them in a healthier way.

I convinced myself that nobody really cared what happened to me. I had no friends, no one to talk to, and my mother was often out drinking 'til all hours. Lots of time I was awake all night worrying about what was going to happen to me. I felt so empty and alone. After awhile I couldn't stand hurting anymore so I withdrew into my own kind of solitary confinement.

One day a guy I knew from school came to see me. At first I tried to get rid of him, but when he told me about himself, I listened. He shared his feelings about living with an alcoholic and told me how Alateen had helped him. He asked me to go to a few meetings with him. I was so desperate that I went with him that night.

I've been going ever since. Mom isn't much better, but I am. Now I have something to fill up that emptiness and I know I never have to be lonely again.

Things to Think About

I'm not alone! What a great feeling to say that and believe it. The program fills up the empty spaces in my life and gives me a reason to live. The people in the fellowship remind me over and over that somebody really cares about me.

I really took my schoolwork to heart. My parents only asked average grades of me, but I expected more of myself. I wasn't interested in learning anything; I just wanted their approval. In time it became an obsession with me. I thought my success in school was the only thing that made me rate as a person. I *needed* to be the best in everything. With that kind of attitude, I made a lot of enemies.

As I look back now, I realize that life then was like existing in a straitjacket. But with the help of Steps Four and Five, I'm learning to overcome that feeling. I'm trying to take myself a little less seriously. I'm starting to see that there's more to me than grades and marks on a report card and I'm beginning to like me as I am, even if I'm not always at the "top of the class."

Things to Think About

Being good at school gives me a nice feeling. But if I cling to that feeling it can be a kind of security blanket. That's when I get into trouble. The program helps me realize that being the best isn't everything; who I am is what really counts.

For a long time I had faith in God. I asked Him for help and He gave it to me. But after awhile, I started to feel that He wasn't living up to my expectations so *I* took control of things. That didn't work out too well either and I had more problems than I'd bargained for.

By working the Twelve Steps and Twelve Traditions, I've found a new kind of faith. It's a "twofold" faith. I have faith in my Higher Power, knowing that His guidance is always there when I need it *and* I have faith in myself, knowing that with God's help I can work out my problems.

Thinking of faith in this way has opened up a whole new world of freedom and growth for me. Problems aren't roadblocks anymore; they're learning experiences that I can use to help me grow "One Day at a Time."

Things to Think About

Facing my problems is the first step toward solving them. From this point on I need faith to help me work out a plan of action. If I have faith in my Higher Power and faith in myself, my problems will open the door to a better life.

Living is growing. With every tick of the clock we change. I'm not the same now as when I was younger. I don't look the same and I think and feel differently. I've learned a lot since then and I can do many more things.

But sometimes I don't think I'm growing fast enough. I get really impatient with myself. I want more. I need to know everything, have everything, and be everywhere all at once.

I'm not very patient with other people, either. If only they'd do what I want them to, things would work out the way I think they should.

When I take time to think about it, I can see that being impatient gets in the way of my growth. I may be growing all the time, but it can only show when I'm patient with myself and the people around me.

Things to Think About

I'm always asking others to be patient with me. A popular saying says it all: "Please be patient with me; God isn't finished with me yet." The program shows me how to be more patient with myself and that helps me to remember that other people might be "unfinished," too.

Many times I feel as though I'm all alone with my problems—that I'm different. In Alateen I've come to realize that the best way to let go of these feelings is to share with other Alateen members.

I need to get together with someone and talk about my feelings. By putting my thoughts into words, I find that I'm not alone. That's one of the greatest things Alateen can offer.

Trusting my Alateen friends is hard to do because I'm not used to sharing my true feelings. But the more I do it, the easier it gets and the more I grow. I have started to find answers to my problems and realize that trusting others is one of the keys to my happiness in the program.

Things to Think About

Trusting other people is hard because my pride gets in the way. It's not easy, but if I talk things out with my Alateen friends, I'll find I'm not alone with my problems. Today I'll trust another person and give myself a chance to feel some of the serenity this program has to offer.

Alateen has given me the kind of freedom I've always wanted. I don't have to carry resentments and guilt feelings around with me, or let them control my thinking all the time the way they used to.

Today I'm free from my past mistakes. Instead of making the same ones over and over again, I can learn from them so I don't have to repeat them.

I'm free to "speak my mind." When I get together with my Alateen friends, I can share my feelings without fear of being laughed at or feeling guilty for standing up for myself.

Now, with the help of the program, I'm free to grow!

Things to Think About

Before Alateen I was like a prisoner. All my bad feelings and past mistakes were locked up tight inside of me. Now I have the freedom to let go of all that. I'm a new person today with a chance to grow and make something of my life.

All of us have problems and troubles. Sometimes we panic and get worked up about things. That's when we need to remember "Easy Does It" and slow down.

But the slogan doesn't suggest that we slow down to a stop! I did. I had jobs to do: washing the dishes, baby-sitting, taking out the garbage, cleaning my room. I didn't like doing them so I'd say, "Easy Does It" and forget about doing anything. I hurt myself because I used the slogan to avoid my responsibilities to my family, friends, and teachers.

I heard an expanded version which I like better: "Easy Does It" (but do it). I can live life at a slower speed and still work on my responsibilities to myself and other people.

Things to Think About

"Easy Does It" doesn't tell me to stand still. It's an action slogan. It keeps me sane, cools me down when I'm about to boil over, and helps me to keep growing at a steady pace.

I tried attending some Al-Anon meetings, along with my regular Alateen meetings, to get an idea of what's in store for me when my time in Alateen is finished. I was a little scared at first, but when the members told me they were glad to see me, I felt right at home.

I kept going back each week and now I have a lot of Al-Anon friends. Some of them are old enough to be my grandmother, but we have a simple and good kind of communication—one person sharing honestly with another, just like it is in Alateen. Age is no barrier because the program is our common bond. It draws us together as we help each other recover and grow.

Things to Think About

Going to Al-Anon meetings help me to realize there *is* a place for me after Alateen. It's a good way to find more friends in the fellowship, but more than that, Al-Anon is a continuation of the great program I found. If I'm looking for more of the special things the program has given me, Al-Anon is the place for me.

Sometimes I think if I tell people I like myself, they'll think I'm bragging. But if I don't like myself, how can I expect other people to like me?

Liking myself doesn't mean I think I'm the greatest or that I'm better than everybody else. It simply means I'm satisfied with what God has given me. If I look inside myself, I'll find the proof—lots of good qualities.

Thanks to the program I can feel good about myself today and accept myself.

Things to Think About

What do I like about myself? When I stop and take a look, I realize I'm full of good stuff. A popular saying tells it like it is: "I'm special because God doesn't make junk."

I live with an alcoholic. Whether he's still drink-ing or not, the situation is too hard for me to handle without help. I need to detach from the problem and not let myself become emotionally involved in it. That's easier said than done!

The program can give me the help I need. I'll start with the Serenity Prayer. The Twelve Steps and Traditions and the slogans will help, too. I'll work the program the best way I know how and try to let go of the things that hurt or upset me.

Things to Think About

When I detach, my mind is clear and things don't "get under my skin." I can relax and be natu-ral. Today I'll stop concentrating on the things that are bothering me and keep my mind on the source of my help—the program.

Fear is something we all experience in one way or another. It can be fear of what tomorrow will bring or bad memories of yesterday.

I used to be so afraid of the future and the past that I couldn't enjoy the present. Now I'm learning to deal with my fears by using the slogan "One Day at a Time." It helps me to stop worrying about the days to come and memories which can't be changed, and reminds me that *today* is the only day I can live. I start to let go of my fears and use the courage which the program gives me to make this day a good one.

Things to Think About

When I let fear of the past or for the future creep into my life, it's hard to work the program to the best of my ability today. Taking life a day at a time puts things back into perspective. It gives me a chance to face my fears with courage and make the most of right now.

I thought I had admitted that I was powerless over my alcoholic mother. But when I started overreacting to her actions again, I wasn't so sure. In fact, I began to doubt whether I'd really taken the First Step at all.

At an Alateen meeting on Step One, I realized what was happening. I *had* taken the First Step, soon after I came to Alateen. But I'd slipped. I thought I'd done it perfectly the first time and I guess I'd just forgotten about it. I found out that it doesn't work that way.

I need to take the First Step again and I'll have to keep taking it for a long time to come. I'm glad about that because now I understand that it's not something I do once and forget about. Like the rest of the program, it's for living and doing each day.

Things to Think About

I can't stop thinking about the program just because I've gone through the Steps one time. I'm human and a long way from being perfect. If I want the program to "sink in," I have to keep working these Steps each day, "One Day at a Time."

Before Alateen my problems were like a pimple. As the infection built up inside me, I started to hurt. If I tried to squeeze out the infection before I was ready, it was very painful. When someone touched me, the pain was even worse.

When I got to Alateen, I found out I wasn't alone, that I wouldn't be criticized or laughed at. I started to trust and open up. The first time I talked, I ached inside, but getting out the built-up infection was a real relief.

If I don't get it all out the first time, I have to keep trying. And when the infection is gone, I have to leave it alone, quit picking at it, and let it heal.

Things to Think About
Problems are painful, but I've got a way to handle them. When I share the hurt and get it outside of myself, the pain starts to go away and the healing begins. Alateen shows me how to *stay* "healthy."

Am I knocking my head against a brick wall trying to change things that can't be changed? Or am I working "One Day at a Time" on me?

If I'm spending my time working at impossible tasks, gritting my teeth, and growling, "I'll never give up!" —I'm probably feeling miserable. That's what comes from being stubborn.

But if I'm trying to hang in there, working for good even when the obstacle is a big one, I'm using "stick-to-it-iveness." That's the special quality that comes from practicing the program "One Day at a Time." It makes me want to keep trying, even when the going gets tough.

Things to Think About

When I'm stubborn, I'm usually fighting so hard with myself that I don't accomplish much. I want things to work out my way—and *now*. But when I use "stick-to-it-iveness," I can tackle my problems one step at a time and enjoy the good feelings that come from trying to do the best I can. Today I'll stop being so stubborn and stick to working the program.

When I talk about Alateen, some people get turned off. It hurts my pride a bit until I remember that some people don't want what the program has to offer.

Step Twelve asks me to "carry the message to others." That much I can do. But I can't be responsible for the way it's received. If people don't want to accept the help that's there for them, that's their choice. All *I* can do is "Let Go and Let God" and hope they find an answer in their own way and time.

Things to Think About

Sometimes I want everybody to have what I've found in the program, but they don't always want it. In Twelfth Step work I'm only a messenger. I carry the message and have to leave the rest in God's hands.

I used to make myself look good on the outside so everyone would think I was special. But inside I was a wreck. I was full of hate; I had no love for anyone. I was jealous of other people and felt sorry for myself. I couldn't let people know the real me so I had to cover it up.

Alateen made me look at my insides. Just being able to talk about my feelings at meetings helped me get a lot of things off my chest. I started to use the Serenity Prayer and the slogans. They helped me accept myself as I was and gave me the courage to make necessary changes in my life.

Today I'm trying to be honest about how I feel inside. I have my share of problems; now I'm working them out with the help of the Twelve Steps and my Alateen friends. I'm still taking care of "the outside," too, but I know I don't have to hide behind a cover anymore.

Things to Think About

In Alateen I recover from the inside out. I don't have to hide behind a mask anymore because everyone can see right through me anyway. I can be honest and face up to the truth about myself. After playing "The Great Cover-up" for so long, it feels good to let the real me out.

Today we may find we're not working our program the way we'd like to. We're going back to our old way of thinking, worrying about things that don't really matter. We bang our head against a stone wall, thinking we're a failure.

Maybe we feel that way because we're not listening to or accepting the message that Alateen is giving to us.

If we listen to the sharing in our Alateen group, keep an open mind, and believe that we can learn something from someone today, we might get back into the swing of things and start working the program again.

Things to Think About

"Listen and Learn": it makes good sense. Using this slogan in my life can help me at home and in school. If I try to pay attention to others, I can learn more about them and myself.

I used to be a follower. I didn't have a lot of confidence in my own opinion so I let other people make up my mind for me. Besides, it took less effort on my part to let others do my thinking for me. Some of the people I was following led me into things I didn't like, but I was so afraid to say anything that I just went along with them. I got into a lot of trouble and felt really miserable inside.

When I came to Alateen, I found people who were looking for answers to their problems. They made it clear that they couldn't give me the answers to mine. I'd have to learn to think for myself and find my own answers in my own way and time. And that's the way it's worked. I'm even starting to make a few decisions for myself. It hasn't been easy turning my back on the people who controlled my life before Alateen. But now I can say, "No," and mean it and feel a lot better because I'm my own person.

Things to Think About

It's tempting to take the easy way out and let others tell me what to do. But how will I ever learn to stand up for myself? The program can help. When I grab hold of the new confidence it gives me, I can decide for myself in what direction I want to travel and start using the Steps to get there.

I had decided that the alcoholic would never get better. But I felt sorry for him and I wanted to stay with him when the rest of the family was ready to walk out. As drunk as he was, my father was great compared to my mother. It almost seemed as if she enjoyed being miserable. I got to the point where I just couldn't stand her anymore and I was looking forward to getting away from her.

Just as everything was falling into place, my mother went to Al-Anon. She didn't change overnight, but I could tell something was different. She started to listen to me and instead of screaming her head off, she talked to me like a human being. I was angry at first; she'd ruined all my plans. But as time went by, I was so impressed with the change in her that when she suggested I try Alateen, I went with no questions asked. That's when I discovered a program to help *me* work on *my* attitudes.

Things to Think About

It's easy to feel sorry for the alcoholic and blame the nonalcoholic for the way he is. But the alcoholic doesn't need my pity and the nonalcoholic doesn't need my blame. Changing my attitude can be the first step toward giving them both what they really need from me—my love and respect.

Before I came to Alateen, I used to make mountains out of molehills. Someone would say something to me. They'd forget it, but I wouldn't. It would keep going round and round in my head until I had built up a good case of self-pity for me and resentment against them. The more I'd think about it, the worse it would get.

If I want to make a mountain out of a molehill, I just have to keep throwing more dirt on it. The program tells me that's a waste of energy. I ask myself, "How Important Is It?" If it seems more important later than when it happened, I realize that I'm making too much of things again and I can put a stop to that.

I have a better perspective on things today. I'm learning to let go of my resentments and I have a lot more time to enjoy life.

Things to Think About

It's a lot easier to get over a molehill than a mountain. And it takes a lot less out of me. Thanks to Alateen, I'm keeping my "mountain climbing" to a minimum.

A lot of my friends feel that depending on a Higher Power is a sign of weakness. They say I'll never be free to make up my own mind about things as long as I believe in a Power greater than myself.

Before Alateen I went along with that kind of thinking. I now see how wrong I was to let other people tell me what I should and shouldn't believe. Faith in a Higher Power is a very personal thing. No one else has the answers for me; I have to find them for myself.

With the help of Step Two and the rest of the program, I'm doing just that. I'm not the kind of weak, mindless person my friends thought I was. In fact, I think I'm a lot stronger because I have a Power behind me and I'm free to explore things in my own time and reach my own conclusions.

Things to Think About

Some people think they have to do everything on their own. I'd rather work together with a reliable source of help, my Higher Power. No matter what other people may say, it takes a lot of courage to put my trust in that Higher Power. Doing this gives me the strength I need to meet each day.

Our Alateen group was large when it started, but there were cliques and after awhile people started to leave for different reasons. The group was unorganized. We never knew who was chairing the meeting each week. Regular members stopped coming and eventually the group became very small.

Then we took a group inventory and discussed group problems. It was like taking Steps Four and Five for the group. We worked at fixing the trouble spots and our group started to grow again.

Today, a lot of people are coming to the group and staying. We have a Step and Tradition meeting once a month and we know who's chairing every week. Best of all, there's a lot of love and friendship in the group again.

Things to Think About

If our group is in trouble, so are we. Facing the problems and doing something about them can help. Keeping our group strong keeps the love and friendship alive and makes it a place where all of us can get the help we need.

I've found a lot of friends in Alateen. Every time I go to a meeting I know I'm going to be among friends. I don't have to be afraid to say anything because I know they've had similar problems and they understand.

When I'm at a meeting, I know if I say something it won't go outside the four walls of that room. When I have a fight with my parents, I can tell the people in my Alateen group and they'll suggest something to help me. We still have fights at home, but I'm slowly learning to cope and to know what to do, thanks to my Alateen friends.

Now, instead of trying to work things out by myself, I can hand over my problems to my Higher Power and work together with people who really care about me.

Things to Think About

My Alateen group gives me the support I need. They're the most honest group of kids I've ever met. They help me when I feel down, when I have a negative attitude, but they also let me know when I do things right. I couldn't ask for a more open and helpful group of friends. Today I'll remember to appreciate them!

How do I handle success? When everything I've worked for begins to happen, when everything seems to click into place, and when I seem to have the right answer at the right time, how do I act?

Do I become so sure I'm always right that I ignore what others have to offer when they share their experiences? Do I demand that others always listen to *me*? Do I fall into the habit of expecting praise and recognition?

Alateen shows me when I'm getting caught up in myself and my success. It helps me to understand that real success is just trying to live the program as well as I can each day.

Things to Think About

"I've got it made!" There's real danger in thinking that way. I can take time to enjoy my recovery, but if I sit around, I'll only slide back into some pretty selfish thinking. Today is my day to move ahead!

If I'm failing in my schoolwork, whose fault is it? Can I blame it on my alcoholic parent? I'd like to, but Alateen won't let me. My studies and grades are *my* responsibility. If I skip classes and avoid studying for tests, I'm not accepting that responsibility.

In Alateen I learned to be responsible by living the Twelve Steps. Instead of blaming my failure and disappointments on other people, I make an honest effort to work my program and start accepting responsibility for my actions.

Things to Think About

I'm here to carry my own load. I'm responsible for finding my own answers and making my own decisions. I have the program to help me do that. If I use it in my life today, I'll learn a lot about being responsible to myself. It's a good way to start growing up!

Newcomer: My friends don't want to come to our house anymore. They say it makes them feel uncomfortable when they see my mother drunk. I don't blame them. I'm ashamed of her myself."

Member: "It used to be that way with me, too, until I realized that my father's illness was no reason for me to be ashamed or embarrassed. I wouldn't feel that way if he had cancer or diabetes, so I don't have to with alcoholism either. If I remember that he's sick, it helps me to understand him a lot better.

"When I started feeling more comfortable with my father, so did my friends, and they started coming back to our house. One of them even asked me how I did it and when I told him about Alateen, he said he'd like to try it because he was having the same problems."

Things to Think About

Alcoholism is an illness. When I try to remember this, I'm not so quick to put the alcoholic down. If I treat the alcoholic with understanding, we're a lot more comfortable with each other and my friends seem to respect him more, too. My attitude makes a big difference; it may even help someone else who has the same kind of troubles.

Do I remember what it was like to come to my first Alateen meeting? I didn't come because it was the fun thing to do; I came because I *had* to. I was angry at everyone and everything. I was going to a meeting where there would be talk about alcoholism when all I wanted was to get alcoholism out of my life. I worried about who would be there and whether or not I could trust them. I was sure they'd laugh at me if I talked and told them how I felt.

Of course none of what I expected was true. But the thoughts were real, just the same. If I try to put these thoughts behind me, I may be forgetting what a help they can be to a newcomer who has just come to our group. They may be the first thing she understands and sharing them may give her a reason to come back and learn how to work the program in her life.

Things to Think About

Past experiences, good and bad, are part of the gift I can give to newcomers. They need to know I've been where they are right now. Remembering my past and sharing it is a way to connect with them. It can open the doors to today for them and show them that someone understands.

When I came to Alateen, I spent a long time learning how to detach from the alcoholic. But I found out there were other people I had to detach from as well. I was a controller, obsessed with the idea of taking care of everything and everyone. I'd always thought the members of my family were too weak and stupid to do anything, so I took over. In school and around the neighborhood, I organized everything and dictated the rules because I was sure no one else knew how.

When I started to lose a lot of friends and my family began to react to me, I realized how much harm I was doing. I wanted to stop controlling other people before I ruined the few relationships I had left. The first three Steps were a big help. First, I had to admit that I had a problem with holding on to things that weren't my business. Second, I came to believe that a Power greater than myself could help me. And third, I asked that Higher Power to take away my problem while I tried to be more positive in my thoughts and actions.

Things to Think About

Detachment isn't something I only do with the alcoholic. I have to let go of others, too, and let them look after their own lives. When I do, I'll discover they know a lot more than I give them credit for, and then I'll have more time to work at being a better friend and family member.

For the longest time I felt the Traditions were only for the group. It wasn't until I was involved in service work that my view of the Traditions changed.

Now I think that the Twelve Traditions are just as important to me as the Twelve Steps. They talk about getting along with people: working together, being a person others can trust, having a purpose, and trying to live by Alateen principles.

It's my responsibility to work the Traditions in my own life. By doing that, I can help make our group strong so all of us can learn to use the whole program.

Things to Think About

The Traditions apply to our groups, but they can help me, too. When problems crop up in my relationships with others, I'll look to the Traditions for help. They'll point me to answers that can make me a stronger person in any situation.

When I came to Alateen I knew nothing about the disease of alcoholism and my part in it. The more I learned, the easier it was to understand and forgive the alcoholic and other members of my family.

Acceptance came in time. Through the help of the program—reading literature, using the Serenity Prayer, the slogans, and the Steps, and by talking out problems with other members—the fog started to lift and I began to love and accept the alcoholic as well as others.

Alateen gave me a chance to learn more about myself, too. As I started to understand some of my thoughts and feelings, I learned to forgive myself. Eventually I began to accept myself just the way I was.

Things to Think About

It's easier to accept something when I know what I'm dealing with. The program helps me to learn more about alcoholism and myself. That makes it easier to accept, understand, and even love my family and myself.

I lived alone with my father. When he was drinking, he would beat me so I spent a lot of time on the street running away from him. Eventually I got caught breaking the law and was sent to a detention center. I tried to act tough, but inside I felt scared and completely alone.

One night some kids from the local Alateen group came to the center to conduct a meeting. When I was forced to go, I tried to act cool. But when the kids shared their feelings, I melted. I started to cry and one of the boys put his arm around me. At first I wanted to pull away, but deep inside it felt good to know that somebody really cared about me. After that, the meetings kept me going from week to week.

When the time came for me to be released, I was scared, but my Alateen friends were there to help me. Once I was settled, they encouraged me to come to their group and I've been there ever since. Things aren't much better at home, but they're a lot better with me. As soon as I can, I want to go back to the center to show guys like me that there's help for them, too.

Things to Think About

Somebody caring about me broke down my walls of loneliness. If I reach out and show others I care, it can do the same for them.

When I was asked to take a position in the group, I let it go to my head. I thought I was really something. My ego got in the way and things really got out of hand. Someone in the group reminded me about Tradition Two. It brought me back to reality and kept me there.

Ever since then, I've realized that I'm a trusted servant of the group—no better and no worse than anyone else. I've been chosen to take on this responsibility because others trust me. I'm expected to serve the group, not make all the decisions. Knowing that helps to keep me humble and the group gets better service from its trusted servant.

Things to Think About

Having a chance to serve my group makes me feel good. If I'm tempted to make a big deal out of it, it might be wise to remember that service is really a special opportunity to do things for others. It doesn't make me more important; it simply means that people trust me to get the job done.

I used to judge everyone by my first impressions. When I'd meet people I didn't like, I'd do my best to avoid them.

After I came to Alateen, I started giving myself a chance to get to know people better. "Keep an Open Mind" made a real difference. I found out that the people I'd been criticizing weren't so bad after all. They had faults, just like me, but nothing that really mattered.

Now I try to look for the best in people. When I don't like people I meet for the first time, I try to give them the benefit of the doubt. It usually works out fine and sometimes we even end up becoming good friends.

Things to Think About

If I'm too quick to judge other people, I'll never have many friends. Trying to "Keep an Open Mind" helps me to be more tolerant and understanding. When I take time to think about the good that's in other people, I'll have a better chance of finding the friends I've always wanted.

We used to have a lot of problems in our group. We talked about the alcoholic instead of trying to help ourselves. Before and after our meetings, when we should have been talking about the program to newcomers, we wasted time fooling around and talked about everything *but* the program.

When things started to go wrong, a lot of people stopped going to meetings instead of trying to make improvements. Our group was ready to fold when someone suggested we take a look at Tradition Five.

Trying to apply it showed us that we have only one purpose: to help each other. We learned that we could do that best by helping ourselves. We stopped taking other people's inventories and started talking about how *we* were feeling. And we spent more time sharing with each other about how the program was helping us.

Today our group is doing better. We still have problems, but everyone, including newcomers, keeps coming back to meetings. Now, because of Tradition Five, we know *why* we come to Alateen.

Things to Think About

Tradition Five tells me why I'm here. I don't have time to talk about anyone else or let myself get sidetracked by other things. I need to concentrate on helping myself and be ready to share with other people. When I do that, I'll help to keep our group going so it can help everyone who comes, including me.

The first time I walked into an Al-Anon meeting, I was scared—afraid that I'd be rejected. I didn't realize until later that they were just as scared as I was; I'm a kid, and kids scare some adults. But as soon as I accepted them and they accepted me, the walls were broken down and things were fine.

I know now that I have something to give to Al-Anon members, just as they have something to give to me. We're all members of the same fellowship and we're trying to work the same program. Instead of looking at them as grownups or parents, I try to "Keep an Open Mind" and remember that Al-Anon members are people—people who need help just like me.

Things to Think About

When I go to an Al-Anon meeting, I have to be ready for some "give and take." I have to let go of my fears and remember that Al-Anons are people too. We all share the same feelings about living with an alcoholic and we're trying to live the same program. We're in this together, helping each other.

I found out in Alateen that alcoholism is a disease. Understanding and accepting this helps me to stop feeling guilty every time my mother blames me for her drinking. She can't be helped until she's ready, until she reaches out for help herself.

I also learned that alcoholism is a *family* disease. I know now that I can't blame my father for my mother's drinking and the rest of our problems. He's trying his best to cope with a tough situation.

Thanks to the program, I can understand both my parents better today and the relationship between us is a lot stronger.

Things to Think About
When I understand that I'm dealing with a disease, I can stop blaming myself and everybody else for the alcoholism in my family. The alcoholic can't be helped until he wants to be, but the help *I* get can keep the lines of communication open between my parents and me.

Before coming to Alateen, I thought my life was hopeless. I was sure no other person could possibly have it worse than me. I did a lot of complaining; nothing ever changed. My father kept telling me I wanted to live in a "storybook" world, but I didn't think I was looking for anything too far out of the ordinary. All I really wanted was a feeling of love.

Now that I'm working the program, I realize that what I want in our home depends on *my* attitude. If I'm looking for love, I have to be willing to show it instead of complaining about not having it. One of the tools that helps me with this is Tradition Eleven. I try to use "attraction rather than promotion." I find I'm a lot happier with what I do and say and it's rubbing off on other people, too.

Things to Think About

When I want my home life to change, sometimes I have to take the lead. I can do that with the help of the Eleventh Tradition. Instead of harping on how things could be better, I can "attract" my family to a new way of life by working the program in *my* life today.

Before Alateen, I thought God was a man who created miracles. He wasn't doing a thing for me so I rejected Him. And I wasn't ashamed of it, either!

When I came to the fellowship I heard the words "Higher Power" and that was great. It took me about two years to find *my* Higher Power. When I did there was a real change in my attitude and my outlook on life was a lot better.

Step Eleven shows me how to stay in touch with my Higher Power and myself. I meditate: I go somewhere by myself and think of who I am, what my values are, and what I'm doing about myself. I try to find out what God's will is for me. Sometimes it's hard, but if I do what I think *He* wants me to do, things will work out best for me and I'll be on the right track.

Things to Think About

The Eleventh Step is a time for thinking and a time for talking with my best friend, my Higher Power. I try to understand what His will is for me and ask for the power to show it in my actions. God's power is go-power.

One of the most important things I learned in Alateen was to put "First Things First." The first thing I needed to work on was me. Instead of trying to change everything about me at once, I took things one at a time. I'm a long way from being finished, but it's getting easier as time goes by.

I know I'll never be perfect, but at least today I can honestly say I feel good about myself. Alateen has helped me realize that even though I'll never be all good, I'm not all bad either.

Things to Think About

Changing myself is a top priority in Alateen. The more I work on myself, the better I'll feel. "First Things First" gives me the push I need to get on with it.

An Alateen member once wrote to his former group telling how he could no longer attend meetings, as there were none near his new home. As the members listened, they realized it was a story of gratitude.

"I didn't realize how much Alateen meant to me until I didn't have it anymore. Sometimes it's really tough. I need the program now more than ever.

"There's no telling where I'd be today if it weren't for the program. I probably would have dropped out of school, run away from home, or started drinking. Instead I have a clearer mind now and I can accept my mother for who she is because I love her. Thank God for Alateen!"

Things to Think About

If I have the chance to attend meetings, I'll try not to take that for granted. If I can't get to meetings, I can still stay in touch with other members by writing to the Lone Member Service at the World Service Office.

I wouldn't make it some days if the Serenity Prayer wasn't around. Especially in those days when everything seems to go wrong. I used to count to ten and then blow up, but now it's different. I use the Serenity Prayer and it gives me a kind of inside peace that helps me to be more patient.

It helps me in a lot of situations: when my dad gets angry at me or when my mom goes on a bender. It took a little while, but I can even use it with my friends now. When I start a fight with one of them, it makes me stop and realize that what I'm arguing about is really stupid.

Most of all the Serenity Prayer has given me the "wisdom to know the difference" between what I was before Alateen and what I am now. There's no comparison and it feels just great!

Things to Think About

I've come a long way since I started using the Serenity Prayer each day. I don't boil over the way I used to. I'm learning to accept problems as they are and face them with the help of my Higher Power. It also helps me change the one thing that I can—*myself*. A sure way to find peace of mind is: the Serenity Prayer.

I used to ask God to help me but only if I really wanted something. When I didn't get everything I thought I should have, I gave up on Him. I figured He had let me down by not answering all my prayers.

Now that I'm in the program, I've come to believe that God really does care about me. I realize that even though I gave up on Him, He never gave up on me. He's always ready to help me if I make an effort to help myself.

I still don't get everything I want, but I know now that what I get is what God thinks I need and that's okay with me.

Things to Think About

God is not unreachable. He's a good friend who never gives up on me. I can talk to Him, not just to ask a favor, but to thank Him and let Him know how things are going for me today.

I could understand why my father was like a Dr. Jekyll and Mr. Hyde: he had a drinking problem. But I couldn't see why my mother was so touchy all the time. She'd be nice one minute and then without warning, she'd be screaming at the top of her lungs. I had a lot on my mind and wanted to talk to her, but it was so hard to know what she'd be like. So I just gave up and stopped going to her.

I really resented my mother when I came to Alateen and it took me a long time to change my attitude. Only after I listened to a lot of people in the same situation did I start to understand the pressure my mother was under. She didn't have alcohol to cover up her feelings the way my father did; she was living on raw nerve. When I realized the position she was in, I actually felt something for her. At first it was hard to show it, but the more I tried, the better I felt. In time, I started sharing my problems with my mother again and we grew closer than we'd ever been before.

Things to Think About

Sometimes I cut myself off from others before I give myself a chance to understand their feelings. It can happen in my family if I don't stop and think about what my nonalcoholic parent is going through. Instead of shutting her out of my life, I'll try to keep the lines of communication open and let her know I care.

I used to try hard to please other people because I wanted them to love me. But I couldn't accept their love and respect because I couldn't love myself. I thought I was useless; a real nothing.

Alateen gave me the hope that I could be a special person. I looked at myself and I found that there was a lot inside of me that I liked.

I feel a lot better about myself today. There are times when I don't take care of myself the way I should, but I'm not so down on myself. I know that I am what I make of myself. The program is helping to make me into someone that I really love and respect.

Things to Think About

Alateen tells me if I don't love myself, it's hard to accept love from other people. Today I know I'm full of all kinds of special, good qualities. I'm learning to love myself and let other people love me.

Before Alateen I was very lonely and frustrated. I tried all kinds of things to escape my problems. I felt as if I was alone in a dark room. I thought there was nothing for me.

I was wrong—there was Alateen. As I attended meetings and shared with other members, I could see small rays of light coming into the darkness. The rays became stronger and stronger as I kept coming to meetings.

I hope one day I'll be able to walk out of that dark room and leave my past troubles locked behind me. I'm grateful today to be one of the luckier teenagers who has Alateen. It's changed my life completely.

Things to Think About

Things are looking up for me thanks to the program. It's a great feeling to have hope and to face the day with a good attitude. Today is another chance to "look on the bright side."

I owe so much to Alateen. Look at what it's given to me: a choice between my old way of thinking and a new and better way of living, a chance to get to know a Higher Power, and a challenge to carry out His will for me.

Maybe I can try, in some small way, to repay Alateen for the benefits I've received. I can do this by welcoming newcomers, by sharing experience, strength, and hope with others, and by turning my life over to the care of God as I understand Him. In a way, it's like working for my Higher Power. And after all, who runs the whole show?

God gave me this terrific program to work and live by. If I want to keep it, I have to give it away.

Things to Think About

Alateen is a new way of life for me. With friends who care and a Higher Power to show me the way, my life has really turned around. Now I can help others who need Alateen, too. It's one way I can repay some of the great things the program has given to me.

When we live with an alcoholic, some of us feel we have no choice but to sit at home and feel sorry for ourselves. Others run away only to find that they're really no happier than before they left. Some even try to escape the problem by using alcohol and drugs.

The program gives us the choice to stay and do something positive about our lives. We learn not to let our problems at home get us down. If things do get bad, we find someone to talk to. We try to make healthy decisions for ourselves and use the program to help us face our problems with courage one day at a time.

Things to Think About

I realize now that living with an alcoholic doesn't have to be a dead end. Life is full of possibilities. If I work on my life, I can live with an alcoholic and still get a lot out of each day.

"We have to accept ourselves before we can accept anyone else." How many times have we heard that at meetings? Accepting ourselves is just as hard as accepting another person—sometimes even harder. But it's very important.

I used to pick out faults in other people that I found in myself. I'd get upset at my family or friends for doing something wrong or for being forgetful. But I'd never stop to think about the times that I'd been wrong or that I'd forgotten something.

Alateen helps me to accept that I'm human. I can't handle everything. I make plenty of mistakes. Accepting this in myself makes it a lot easier for me to accept faults in other people, too.

Things to Think About

Today I'll try to accept myself as I am—good and bad together. I'll be patient with myself and take things as they come. This will help me to accept other people for what they are: human beings just like me.

Not long ago I learned a lesson in humility. I met a newcomer at a meeting and we seemed to hit it off. We agreed to stay in touch with each other and when I called her a couple of times, I expected her to call me back. She didn't and I was disappointed. When I found out she'd called someone else, my pride was hurt.

Then I realized I was trying to control her life. She's free to talk to anybody she wants. I have answers, but I'm not the only person she can learn from. Maybe what I have to say isn't what she needs to hear right now.

Because I let go, we're good friends today. I'm happy for her that she's getting the help she needs from others and I'm glad that I had a chance to learn an important lesson.

Things to Think About

I'd like to help every newcomer who comes to our group. I *can* help some, but I don't have the answers for everybody. When I let others carry the message, it spreads around the responsibility and helps to build a solid foundation for sponsorship in the group. There's no better way to keep new people coming back!

I always was a loner. I thought everybody wanted me out of the way so I stayed off by myself. It hurt a lot, but not nearly as much as the pain of being laughed at or told to get lost when I tried to mix with others.

By the time I reached Alateen, I was sick and tired of being left out. That's why the warm, open welcome I got when I came was so important to me. It said right away that people wanted me to join in. If they'd kept to themselves in little cliques waiting for me to make the first move, I may never have come back.

Today I know I'm in the right place. I'm always on the lookout for newcomers who seem shy and lonely. There are plenty of them. I want them to have the warm welcome I had so they'll stay, too.

Things to Think About

After years of being cut off from everybody, it's good to be part of something. That's one of the secrets of the fellowship: People want to stay around because of the warm and caring welcome they receive. I want to be a part of this in case others are feeling alone and left out.

I was always harder on myself than I was on other people. I could accept others when they made a mistake, but I expected more of myself.

It got to be a real problem. I couldn't be wrong because that would blow the image I had of myself. It was as if I were standing over my own right shoulder with a big stick ready to knock myself over the head if I stepped out of line.

It's better today. With slogans like "Easy Does It" and the Twelve Steps, I'm learning to go easier on myself and that it's no big deal to be wrong. I'm also starting to see that I can learn a lot from the mistakes I make.

Things to Think About

I expect a lot of myself, but I have to be fair. I *do* have the right to be wrong. When I give myself that kind of freedom, the mistakes I make can be some of the best learning experiences in my life.

I've been around Alateen for quite awhile, but it's only recently that I realize I've really never been a part of it. I'm glad I hit my bottom because I might never have started working the program if I didn't. The Steps have unlocked so many doors that I never believed could be opened. There's an answer to all my problems in them and they've given me direction to my life.

I've found a faith in a Higher Power, too, and I think that's the key to *my* working the program. Believing in that Higher Power lights up my whole world. Sometimes I block out the light because my self-will stands in the way. That's when I get in trouble with myself. Even in those low times I know my Higher Power is still there. I never walk alone when I've got this program and that's a great feeling to have.

Things to Think About

I'm glad I finally woke up and realized how important the program is to me. It's given me a new picture of my life. When I try to make the program part of everything I do, I don't feel as alone anymore and things seem to work out better than I ever expected.

Before I came to Alateen I thought my father was weak—I was sure he could stop drinking if he really wanted to. I thought he was causing the family arguments and the hate we had for each other.

After joining Alateen, I started to understand that alcoholism is a disease. I learned that I couldn't plead or threaten to make him stop drinking. I also learned not to feel guilty for his actions.

I used to blame my low marks, not having any friends, and a lot of other things on my father's drinking. Thanks to Alateen I know *I* am responsible for those things.

Things to Think About

When I learn that alcoholism is an illness, a lot of things fall into place. Even though the alcoholic says and does things that hurt me, I realize a lot of these actions are a part of his illness. Knowing this helps me begin to let go and deal with the pain so I can go on with living today.

I used to think I wanted someone to take care *of* me. Now I know I just wanted someone to care *about* me. Before Alateen I was sure no one did and I felt lonely and depressed.

Because of the fellowship I have people who really *do* care about me. Their friendship is one of my most valuable possessions. When I feel bad and start to think, "No one cares," I remember them. I think about how I can talk to them and say what's really bothering me. They take me for what I am no matter what I've done and they try to help me and share with me every day.

Things to Think About

Without friends it's easy to stay confused and unhappy. But when someone cares for me, I don't feel alone anymore. It means a lot to me to have friends in Alateen. I know they care about me and I think they're glad I care about them, too.

In Step One I'm supposed to admit that I'm powerless over alcohol. How can I do that when I don't even drink?

This Step really means I have no control over alcohol or the alcoholic. I can't do anything about how much he drinks, why he drinks, or what happens when he drinks. In fact, I can't control any person's life but my own.

I'm also asked to admit that my life has become unmanageable. When I look at the way I've been living, I know that's true. I'm not trying as hard in school. I don't bring friends home anymore, and I say things that I don't really mean. I'm letting the situation at home run my life and *I* no longer have any control over me.

Accepting Step One can be the start to finding that self-control again.

Things to Think About

Step One is a good beginning and the rest of the program will help *me* take care of myself. I've let situations and other people control me for too long. This is the day I can take control of my own life.

A young child has a kind of innocent faith in a parent. If she's on a swing, she has the faith that her father will not let her fall. She trusts him. If she does fall, she may not get on the swing for a long time because she's afraid her father will let her fall again. It may take awhile for her to gain back her trust and faith.

When I came to Alateen, I was like that child. I found it hard to have faith after being let down so many times; I needed a reason to believe. I was always asking, "Why?"

With the help of the Second Step, I've found the courage to trust again. I believe in a Power greater than myself. It's not important that I put a name on this Power, just that I believe it will work for me every day.

Things to Think About

Sometimes I need to have the faith of a young child. Step Two asks me to believe—nothing more, nothing less. If I'm willing to do that, and let go of my doubts and fears, it will be a beginning. Today I'll trust in a Power greater than myself and hope that Power will show me the way.

Some of us have a hard time with the Third Step because we can't "Let Go and Let God." We hang on to our old ideas. We think God is waiting for us to make mistakes so He can punish us. Or we believe that God wants us to suffer by living with an alcoholic. Maybe we're just too scared to trust.

In Step Three we find a four-letter word which makes a big difference. We turn our will and our life over to the *care* of God as we understand Him. A Higher Power is like a friend who really cares about us and wants to share our problems. When we know that, we can let go of old ideas. It's a lot easier to trust a friend with our lives and have the faith that things will work out for the best.

Things to Think About

Letting go is easier when I remember that my Higher Power cares about me. He's my friend, through the good times and the bad. He'll be with me today, and every day, to help me.

We come to Alateen to learn how to live comfortably in a home that has been affected by alcoholism. We carry a lot of fears and hurts. Many of us have given up trusting other people.

Alateen helps us to find that trust again. We can talk about our pain to others who understand and we can ask questions without being made to feel dumb. We know that what we say at meetings won't be repeated. This kind of anonymity protects us. By practicing it we learn to trust others and others start to trust us.

Things to Think About

I feel safe in Alateen because I trust the people I'm with. I can say what's on my mind and know that no one is going to spread it around. We all get a lot of help that way, so it's my responsibility to protect the anonymity of others.

I've been in Alateen for only a short time and already I feel like I belong. I'm part of a group of people who understand and love each other. I'm able to cope with my troubles because of the sharing, caring, and hope Alateen members give me. Instead of looking at the past or into the future, I can now live "One Day at a Time."

Some of the members are my closest friends and they help me feel good about myself. At this mixed-up time of being a teenager, with everybody looking for a place to belong, I'm really grateful I have Alateen.

Things to Think About

Everybody wants to feel they fit in somewhere. I've found my place in Alateen. I know I belong because of the good feeling I have when I'm with my Alateen friends. They make me feel wanted and accepted—that's one of the things that keeps me coming back.

I was an expert at saying yes. I wanted everybody to like me so I agreed to do things for others, even if I didn't have the time or know what I was doing. Eventually I got so worn out that I wished I could say *no* more often. But wishing didn't change a thing.

It took the program to help me develop the ability to say "No." Actually, how I felt about myself was the real problem. As I worked on the inventory Steps, I gained a little confidence in myself and realized that I had to start saying "Yes" to myself if I was going to change and make something of my life.

Now when I'm asked to do something, I take some time to think about it. If I can honestly do something to help, I'm glad to say "Yes." If I can't, or if I'm strapped for time, I can say "No" without feeling guilty. I have my self-respect now and that's what really counts.

Things to Think About

If I have trouble saying "No," I have a problem with me. I can do something to change it, if I'm willing to use Steps Four and Five to work on my attitude towards myself. I don't want to say "No" all the time, but I do want to be comfortable enough with me that I can choose when to say "Yes" and when to say "No."

Before I started going to meetings, I couldn't talk about my father being an alcoholic without getting upset and crying. I thought I was stupid, so I tried to hide my feelings and pretended that I didn't feel anything.

I learned in the program that it's okay to get upset; it's not stupid or something to be ashamed of. It's a natural thing. And I don't have to say I don't feel anything, because I do—that's a part of what makes me a person.

I still cry and get upset; I get mad and lose my temper. But I'm learning to control myself a bit more now as I try to be honest about how I feel.

Things to Think About

Feelings aren't right or wrong—they just are. They're a special part of me. Alateen gives me the freedom to feel and the chance to share my real feelings with others who understand.

One evening an Alateen member shared her thoughts about worry with her group:

"Once my mother yelled at me for something I didn't do. She said she was so angry she was going to get drunk. I got upset and left the house. But while I was gone, I worried the whole time about what I'd find when I came home.

"When I finally returned, I was relieved to see that she wasn't drunk. But the next day I had an important test and I didn't do very well. I'd been so busy worrying the night before, I didn't have time to study.

"Now I know I can't afford to worry about whether or not my mother is going to get drunk; that's her decision. I can turn to my Higher Power and use the Serenity Prayer so I don't have to waste time worrying about things I can't control.

Things to Think About

It's no use worrying about whether or not an alcoholic is going to drink. I can't control things like that. Instead I'll concentrate on the important things in my life and make better use of my time today.

At one time I'd argue and lash out instead of taking time to think. It got me into a lot of trouble. I said things in anger and then wished I hadn't. I hurt innocent people with my words and actions and I did many things which I regretted later.

Now, with the help of Alateen, I'm starting to "Think" before I speak and there's not as much hassle in my life. By thinking about the consequences of my actions. I'm learning not to say and do things I'll be sorry for later.

Thinking things over instead of just reacting is really helping to calm me down.

Things to Think About

A lot of my problems could be prevented if I'd simply stop and "Think." When I feel trouble brewing, I'll use this slogan to keep cool and "Think" before I act. That will give me a better chance to concentrate on my own peace of mind.

God is like a super playwright who, as His own stage director, is trying to organize us all into a great production. Each of us has an individual part to play and He's patiently waiting for us to cooperate with each other and follow His script.

Most of us are too busy to listen. We try to act out our own ideas instead of His and we end up doing a lot of worrying and arguing. But God is calm, cool, and collected, absolutely sure that everything will turn out all right.

When we start practicing the Eleventh Step, we learn to sit down, listen, and work along with His directions. Somehow things work out a lot better. We're calmer and happier when we improve our conscious contact with God and follow the original script.

Things to Think About

When I try to run my own life, I mess things up. Step Eleven shows me how to take directions from a better manager. Today I'll listen to my Higher Power and try to live the part He chooses for me.

I have two friends, their names: "Yes But" and "What If." With their help, I can sit back and forget about working the program.

"Yes But" gives me a reason to reject everything I hear. When someone says something that makes good sense and suggests that I try it in my life, all I have to do is call on my friend "Yes But" to find a reason why it would never work for me.

"What If" is a real help, too. Whenever I start to feel like trying something new, my friend makes sure that I'm full of doubt and fear so that I don't have to take any risks.

Having friends like "Yes But" and "What If" is a sure way to keep myself from growing.

Things to Think About

How many times have I used "Yes But" and "What If" as excuses for not really trying to live the program? If I want to make more of my life, I'll "Keep an Open Mind" and have the courage to apply what I hear at my meetings instead of taking the easy way out.

Step Twelve talks about a "spiritual awakening." It doesn't have to be a big thing; it can be as simple as a change in myself, noticing things about myself that I really didn't know before. It's like waking up to a new feeling about myself.

A spiritual awakening comes from trying to practice the Twelve Steps of the program one day at a time. I can keep these tools sharpened by living an honest life and facing things squarely. But the best way for me to keep growing is to reach out. Helping others helps me a lot. My problems don't seem nearly so big when I concentrate on helping other people.

Things to Think About

Twelfth Step work is giving the program away. It's like eating an orange. If I just eat the orange and throw away the seeds, I'll soon be hungry again. But if I plant the seeds, other orange trees will grow and there will be plenty of oranges for myself and others.

GOD GRANT ME THE SERENITY—Easy to say, but this special peace of mind is very hard to achieve. I can't manufacture it myself. As hard as I try to force myself to relax, I can't find real peace of mind without help.

I need God's gift of serenity TO ACCEPT THE THINGS I CANNOT CHANGE—especially other people. Accepting something I disagree with or don't understand is tough. It hurts to sit back and watch those I love destroy themselves when I can't do anything about it.

The acceptance seems to come more easily when I start to understand alcoholism and realize that no one can be helped until they're ready. Nothing I can do will make that time come more quickly. If I "Let Go and Let God" take care of them, I'll be in better shape to help if and when the time does arrive.

Things to Think About

When I say the Serenity Prayer, I ask God to give me a kind of calmness. It helps me to accept the fact that I can't change the alcoholic or others and the way they're living their lives. Today I'll accept the things I can't change and get on with living my own life.

God's gift of serenity gives me COURAGE TO CHANGE THE THINGS I CAN. I can't change anyone else, but I can change myself and my attitude.

Sometimes I'm afraid to take charge of my own life. I don't want to fail. Who do I blame for my mistakes? No one but me!

Alateen helps me to take responsibility for my life. It gives me a program of living that helps me to change and have confidence in myself. It surrounds me with good friends who love me and a Higher Power who guides me and takes good care of my life.

I want to change. I may fail at first, but if I let go and listen to my Higher Power, I'll get all the help I need to put my life in order.

Things to Think About

As much as I'd like to change things and people around me, I'm the only one I can change. It's not easy; I've taken a long time to get to where I am now and I can't change overnight. But with God's help I can make a start today.

Before Alateen I spent most of my time trying to change things I couldn't change and ignoring the things that I could change. I was confused and worn out.

How do I know what I can and cannot change? Sometimes I have to take a chance and trust that God will give me the wisdom to know.

Thanks to the Serenity Prayer, I'm starting to find THE WISDOM TO KNOW THE DIF-FERENCE. It's a real energy-saver. Now, instead of trying to change others, I can accept people and things around me and learn to live with them. That gives me a lot more energy and time to do what Alateen says I'm here to do: change myself.

Things to Think About

The program helps me to accept the things I cannot change. It gives me the tools to change the things I can. I need the wisdom to know the dif-ference. That comes from God's gift of serenity. I'll ask Him for it today.

When I'm jealous, I see only what I want to see in others and in myself. In *their* lives I see all the good things they have; in *my* life, only what I don't have. In both cases I see only what *I want to see* instead of the whole picture.

Jealously is a lot like self-pity. It makes me feel selfish and self-centered.

But I know I can change. I need to see things *as they really are*. The key is to think more about the good things in my own life. That will help me to be happier with what I have and I'll be able to appreciate the good things in the lives of others.

Things to Think About

I cheat myself when I'm jealous of other people. I always come out a loser. The program shows me how to feel better about myself and that helps me to "Live and Let Live." Today I'll try to "count *my* blessings" and be fair to myself and others.

I used to count on the promises the alcoholic
made to me. I'd get all excited about doing
something we planned, only to be crushed when
he'd come home late and say he'd forgotten. I felt
bad, but I kept those feelings all bottled up inside
me and they turned into resentment and distrust.

The program has helped me to understand that
broken promises can be a part of the alcoholic's
sickness. I don't count on things so much now and
I don't feel so disappointed. If the alcoholic makes
a promise, I try to remember he means it at the
time. But if he doesn't keep his promise, I try to
understand and go on with something else instead
of moping around.

Things to Think About

Promises, promises—a lot of the broken ones
made me think the alcoholic didn't care. I know
now that's not true. The alcoholic may want to
keep his promises, but he can't because of his
problem. Today I'll try to remember that broken
promises don't have to break up our relationship.

By the time I got to Alateen, I was sick and tired of playing referee during the fights between my parents. I thought it was my duty to get involved, but I always seemed to get caught in the crossfire. If I tried to help my mother explain her side, my father would beat me up. If I tried to defend my father, my mother would scream and yell at me. Eventually I was so confused and hurt, that I didn't know which way to turn.

That's why I'm so grateful for the First Step and the idea of detachment. Solving my parents' problems isn't *my* responsibility. When they have a fight today, I step back and let them work things out between themselves. It saves me from a lot of bumps and bruises and gives me more time to take care of my own problems.

Things to Think About

Caught in the middle between two angry people isn't a great place to be. Thanks to the program I don't have to put myself in that position anymore. When I stop thinking I have to get involved in everyone else's business, I'll be well on my way to learning how to detach. Then, I'll have a lot more time to concentrate on what really is my business—my own life.

What brought me to Alateen? I wanted to be loved. I was frustrated and lonely and I thought everyone was cared for except me. I came to *get* something.

I did get the love I was looking for. People cared about me and shared their feelings with me. But I learned that "getting" depends a lot on my willingness to *give* and to help others.

Today I realize that if I want to keep getting what I need from the program, I have to "give it away."

Things to Think About

I can't keep what I don't give away. It seems funny, but it's true about the program. "Giving it away" means sharing my experience, strength, and hope, getting involved in my group, volunteering to take on a job, and staying in touch with a newcomer. Most of all it's simply being an active member of Alateen.

Sometimes, as Alateens, we feel that we're not part of the Al-Anon fellowship. What can we do to help bring Alateen and Al-Anon closer together?

We can help by trying to practice the Twelve Steps and Twelve Traditions in our own lives, by sharing our experience, strength, and hope with Al-Anon members at open meetings, by getting involved in our group, district, or area, and by listening to and talking with members whenever we can.

Alateen is part of Al-Anon. We share the same program because we're all trying to learn to live with problems caused by alcoholism. We also share the responsibility for making our fellowship strong and united so that all of us, Alateen and Al-Anon together, can find the help we need.

Things to Think About

As an Alateen member, I'm part of a family—the Al-Anon Family Groups. While we have differences, I'll try to keep in mind all the things that makes us the same and try to do my part to keep us united. The best way I can do that is to keep working on myself and sharing with Alateen *and* Al-Anon members around me.

Before Alateen I kept everything bottled up inside of me. I didn't want anyone to know how I was feeling. It seemed easier to keep it inside than to tell somebody how I felt.

In Alateen I learned to let out my feelings and accept them for what they are. I started by accepting myself as mixed-up and then moved on from there.

Today I'm learning to handle my feelings as I place them in their proper perspective and deal with them instead of allowing them to make my life miserable.

Things to Think About

I trust my Alateen friends. I share my real feelings with them and they help me to accept myself as I am. Thanks to them, I'm starting to relax and find ways to untie some of the knots in my feelings.

Did I come to Alateen looking for a way to get the alcoholic to stop drinking? If I did, I soon learned I couldn't do that, no matter how hard I tried.

The best I can do is to help myself by learning as much as I can about alcoholism. I'll read some Alateen and Al-Anon literature every day and go to my Alateen meetings as often as I can. I'll share my feelings with people who understand and try to let go of the thoughts and actions that hurt me.

Things to Think About

I can help the alcoholic, and my whole family, by helping myself. Changing my attitude might be the thing which encourages the alcoholic to look for help. But even if it doesn't, I won't let that stop me from doing everything I can to better myself.

Looking back and remembering what I was like when I first came to Alateen makes me realize how grateful I am to the program. Friends in the fellowship, my Higher Power, and even my family have helped and I'm thankful to them all.

In a special way, I'm grateful to myself, too, because I'm the one who allowed me to change. That was no easy job! I now know that I'm human and admitting this is a big relief. I make mistakes, but I realize that I'm still okay in spite of them. I can even like and accept myself as I am.

I've also started to show my feelings instead of keeping them locked up inside me. I can love, be angry, and cry if I want to because I make the choice about how I feel and how I deal with the situations in my life each day. I've come a long way and it feels good to know that I've been a big part of making the changes in me.

Things to Think About

I have a lot be grateful for in my new way of life. I owe a great deal to other people, but I can be thankful to myself as well. I'm a better person today because I'm giving myself a chance to let the program work in my life.

THE SERENITY PRAYER

This prayer is read at most group meetings and often analyzed in group discussions. It also serves as inspiration to individuals in daily meditation.

> God grant me the serenity
> To accept the things I cannot change,
> Courage to change the things I can,
> And wisdom to know the difference.

THE SLOGANS OF AL-ANON

These slogans are used in the same way as the Serenity Prayer, to seek spiritual guidance in dealing with our conflicts and challenges. Groups use the slogans as subjects for meetings; individuals use them as reminders in times of stress.

Listed below are the slogans in this book:

> "But for the Grace of God"
> "Easy Does It"
> "First Things First"
> "How Important Is It?"
> "Just for Today"
> "Keep an Open Mind"
> "Keep It Simple"
> "Let Go and Let God"
> "Let It Begin With Me"
> "Listen and Learn"
> "Live and Let Live"
> "One Day at a Time"
> "Think"
> "Together We Can Make It"

TWELVE STEPS

1. We admitted we were powerless over alcohol—
   that our lives had become unmanageable.

2. Came to believe that a Power greater than
   ourselves could restore us to sanity.

3. Made a decision to turn our will and our lives
   over to the care of God *as we understood
   Him.*

4. Made a searching and fearless moral inventory
   of ourselves.

5. Admitted to God, to ourselves, and to another
   human being the exact nature of our wrongs.

6. Were entirely ready to have God remove all
   these defects of character.

7. Humbly asked Him to remove our shortcomings.

8. Made a list of all persons we had harmed, and
   became willing to make amends to them all.

9. Made direct amends to such people wherever
   possible, except when to do so would injure
   them or others.

10. Continued to take personal inventory and
    when we were wrong promptly admitted it.

11. Sought through prayer and meditation to
    improve our conscious contact with God *as we
    understood Him*, praying only for knowledge
    of His will for us and the power to carry that
    out.

12. Having had a spiritual awakening as the result of these steps, we tried to carry this message to others, and to practice these principles in all our affairs.

TWELVE TRADITIONS
OF ALATEEN

Our group experience suggests that the unity of the Alateen Groups depends upon our adherence to these Traditions:

1. Our common welfare should come first; personal progress for the greatest number depends upon unity.

2. For our group purpose there is but one authority—a loving God as He may express Himself in our group conscience. Our leaders are but trusted servants; they do not govern.

3. The only requirement for membership is that there be a problem of alcoholism in a relative or friend. The teenage relatives of alcoholics, when gathered together for mutual aid, may call themselves an Alateen Group provided that, as a group, they have no other affiliation.

4. Each group should be autonomous, except in matters affecting other Alateen and Al-Anon Family Groups or AA as a whole.

5. Each Alateen Group has but one purpose: to help other teen-agers of alcoholics. We do this by practicing the Twelve Steps of AA *ourselves* and by encouraging and understanding the members of our immediate families.

6. Alateens, being part of Al-Anon Family Groups, ought never endorse, finance or lend our name to any outside enterprise, lest prob-

lems of money, property and prestige divert us from our primary spiritual aim. Although a separate entity, we should always cooperate with Alcoholics Anonymous.

7. Every group ought to be fully self-supporting, declining outside contributions.

8. Alateen Twelfth Step work should remain forever nonprofessional, but our service centers may employ special workers.

9. Our groups, as such, ought never be organized; but we may create service boards or committees directly responsible to those they serve.

10. The Alateen Groups have no opinion on outside issues; hence our name ought never be drawn into public controversy.

11. Our public relations policy is based on attraction rather than promotion; we need always maintain personal anonymity at the level of press, radio, films, and TV. We need guard with special care the anonymity of all AA members.

12. Anonymity is the spiritual foundation of all our Traditions, ever reminding us to place principles above personalities.

TWELVE CONCEPTS
OF SERVICE

The Twelve Steps and Traditions are guides for personal growth and group unity. The Twelve Concepts are guides for service. They show how Twelfth Step work can be done on a broad scale and how members of a World Service Office can relate to each other and to the groups, through a World Service Conference, to spread Al-Anon's message worldwide.

1. The ultimate responsibility and authority for Al-Anon world services belongs to the Al-Anon groups.
2. The Al-Anon Family Groups have delegated complete administrative and operational authority to their Conference and its service arms.
3. The right of decision makes effective leadership possible.
4. Participation is the key to harmony.
5. The rights of appeal and petition protect minorities and insure that they be heard.
6. The Conference acknowledges the primary administrative responsibility of the Trustees.
7. The Trustees have legal rights while the rights of the Conference are traditional.
8. The Board of Trustees delegates full authority for routine management of Al-Anon Headquarters to its executive committees.

9. Good personal leadership at all service levels is a necessity. In the field of world service the Board of Trustees assumes the primary leadership.

10. Service responsibility is balanced by carefully defined service authority and double-headed management is avoided.

11. The World Service Office is composed of selected committees, executives and staff members.

12. The spiritual foundation for Al-Anon's world services is contained in the General Warranties of the Conference, Article 12 of the Charter.

(see Warranties, page 374)

GENERAL WARRANTIES
OF THE CONFERENCE

In all proceedings the World Service Conference of Al-Anon shall observe the spirit of the Traditions:

1. that only sufficient operating funds, including an ample reserve, be its prudent financial principle;

2. that no Conference member shall be placed in unqualified authority over other members;

3. that all decisions be reached by discussion vote and whenever possible by unanimity;

4. that no Conference action ever be personally punitive or an incitement to public controversy;

5. that though the Conference serves Al-Anon it shall never perform any act of government; and that like the fellowship of Al-Anon Family Groups which it serves, it shall always remain democratic in thought and action.

INDEX

This index can be a key for individuals seeking help with a particular part of their recovery. It may also provide groups with some starting points for discussions at meetings.

T

Al-Anon Books:

Alateen—Hope for Children of Alcoholics (B-3)

The Dilemma of the Alcoholic Marriage (B-4)

The Al-Anon Family Groups—Classic Edition (B-5)

One Day at a Time in Al-Anon (B-6), Large Print (B-14)

Lois Remembers (B-7)

Al-Anon's Twelve Steps & Twelve Traditions (B-8)

Alateen—a day at a time (B-10)

As We Understood... (B-11)

...In All Our Affairs: Making Crises Work for You (B-15)

Courage to Change—One Day at a Time in Al-Anon II (B-16), Large Print (B-17)

From Survival to Recovery: Growing Up in an Alcoholic Home (B-21)

How Al-Anon Works for Families & Friends of Alcoholics (B-22)

Courage to Be Me—Living with Alcoholism (B-23)

Paths to Recovery—Al-Anon's Steps, Traditions, and Concepts (B-24)

Living Today in Alateen (B-26)

Hope for Today (B-27), Large Print (B-28)

Opening Our Hearts, Transforming Our Losses (B-29)

Discovering Choices (B-30)

NOTES

NOTES